Contents

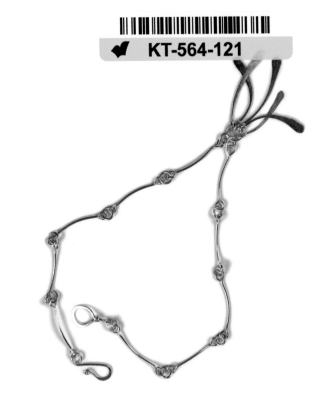

Introduction

For as long as I can remember, I have been drawing, painting, and making things. My parents always said that, as a little girl, I was most happy when I was "fiddling." Now that I'm older and slightly wiser, I'm still fiddling—this time with wire and beads!

I came to jewelry making relatively late in my career, and to wire and bead jewelry design even later. I spent my early childhood in East and West Africa, where various colorful cultures and their artifacts and handicrafts fueled my creativity. Then, having spent a year traveling around Indonesia learning the art of batik making, I completed an art foundation course in England. But it wasn't until I was in my 30s, and stuck in an office job, that I decided to take the plunge and go back to art college to study jewelry design, specializing in metal work and enameling. I was in my element!

A few years later, I found myself as a single mother with two young sons to support, struggling to sell my jewelry at local craft fairs and making one-off commissions whenever they came my way. It was then that I turned to teaching to supplement my income, setting up workshops and demonstrating wire and bead techniques. When people realized that pieces could be designed and created without investing in expensive machinery and equipment, these workshops soon became popular. No soldering, chemicals, or highly skilled processes were required, as wire jewelry can be made with a

The Complete Guide to
Wire & Beaded Jewelry

Over 50 beautiful projects
and variations using
wire and beads

LINDA JONES

CICO BOOKS

LONDON NEW YORK

Published in 2009 by CICO Books
An imprint of Ryland Peters & Small
20–21 Jockey's Fields   341 E 116th St
London WC1R 4BW   New York, NY 10029
www.rylandpeters.com

US: 20 19 18 17 16 15 14 13 12
UK: 10 9 8 7 6 5 4 3 2 1

A CIP catalog record for this book is available from
the Library of Congress and the British Library.

ISBN: 978 1 906525 70 5

Printed in China

Editor: Sarah Hoggett
Designer: Roger Daniels
Photographers: Caroline Arber, Geoff Dann,
Jacqui Hurst, and Gloria Nicol

These projects were first published in the following titles:
Creating Wire and Beaded Jewelry by Linda Jones (CICO Books, 2004)
Making Colorful Wire & Beaded Jewelry by Linda Jones (CICO Books, 2006)
Wire & Bead Celtic Jewelry by Linda Jones (CICO Books, 2007)
Bead & Wire Jewelry for Special Occasions by Linda Jones (CICO Books, 2007)

minimum of fuss and mess at your kitchen table. Fortunately for me, my courses and classes coincided with the emergence of new materials for the craft and hobby market: suddenly, it seemed that beautiful beads and colored wires were everywhere!

As many of my students have discovered, making wire jewelry brings out your creativity. For me, that's the greatest joy. I've met many people who believed that they had no artistic skill, but who have suddenly discovered, through making jewelry, that they do have the ability to create interesting shapes and color combinations—and the boost that gives to their self-confidence is phenomenal! Combine that with the satisfaction of making pieces that are completely different to any of the mass-produced designs in the chain stores, and it's no wonder that the subject has such a wide-ranging appeal. I'm sure that any of you who have already tried making wire jewelry will agree how addictive it can be.

Wire and beaded jewelry is also relatively inexpensive, yet stylish pieces can be created with just three basic pliers, a spool of wire, a sprinkling of beads, and a minimum of fuss. It is great fun to do and even beginners can create beautiful pieces. In fact, I always say that if you can tie your own shoelaces, you've got all the skills needed to learn wire jewelry making!

This book brings together many of my favorite designs that I've created over the years. There are projects to suit all ages. Whether you're looking for a simple piece to wear at work or a more elaborate design for a really special occasion, I'm sure you'll find plenty that catches your eye. All the projects are designed to be fast and fun to create, and you can adapt them to suit your own personal style and taste by using different-colored beads and wires. I hope that they will inspire and trigger the creative artist within you!

LINDA JONES

SHAPING AND TWISTING WIRE:
The Basics

The first thing you need to do when you take up a new craft is to familiarize yourself with the materials at your disposal. The projects in this chapter demonstrate several methods of shaping wire, including bending it into interesting shapes, as in the Squiggle Ring on page 18, winding it around a jig or a dowel to create regular-shaped patterns (Celtic Cross, page 22, and Art Deco Necklace, page 26), curling it around itself to form coils and spirals (Bead Spray Brooch, page 14, and the Double Spiral Necklace, page 36), and creating intricate-looking loops (Floating Amethyst Necklace, page 10). You will also learn how to anchor beads by twisting wire around a stem, as in the Falling Leaves Necklace on page 32 and the Beaded Scarf Slide on page 40, and how to create a frame for a necklace or bracelet by twisting several wires together, as in the Spiral Choker on page 44.

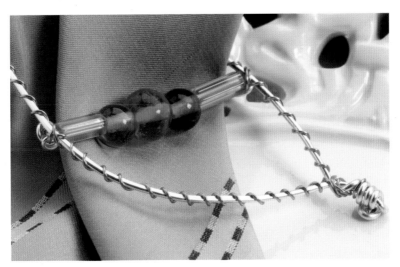

Daytime Delights

Whether your standard daytime wear is a casual pair of jeans and a T-shirt or a smart, tailored suit for the office, every outfit can be transformed by the addition of a simple piece of well-made jewelry. This chapter features a range of everyday brooches, rings, and necklaces to suit all ages, from glamorous girl about town to gorgeous granny!

Floating Amethyst Necklace

Semi-precious stones always look special and, with so many different colors available, you can coordinate them to go with any outfit in your closet. In this necklace, small groups of amethyst chips are strung on nylon filament, so that they appear almost to be floating in thin air. Amethysts are also a birthstone: associated with February birthdays, the purple color is symbolic of wisdom and knowledge. The Birthstone Chart on page 57 sets out which stone or bead color is linked to each month of the year.

OPPOSITE *The natural beauty of the amethyst chip stones gives this necklace and earrings set a classic, timeless quality.*

YOU WILL NEED

- Amethyst chips
- 20-gauge (0.8 mm) silver wire
- 0.5 mm nylon filament
- Approx. 40 x 5 mm silver crimp beads
- Round-, chain-, and flat-nose pliers
- Wire cutters
- Hammer and steel stake

1 Working from a spool of 20-gauge (0.8 mm) silver wire and using your round-nose pliers, curl a complete circle at the end of the wire.

2 Move the pliers next to the first loop and form another loop directly beside it, wrapping the wire around the same section of the pliers so that the loops are roughly the same size.

3 Make a third loop in the same way, then cut the wire off the spool. Repeat steps 1–3 to make a second three-loop unit.

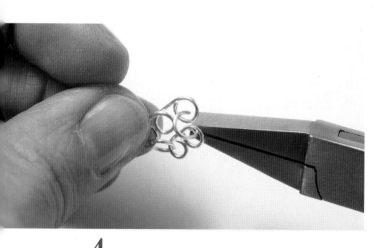

4 Repeat steps 1 and 2 to make two two-loop units. Make two small jump rings from 20-gauge (0.8 mm) silver wire (see page 182). Using the jump rings, attach each two-loop unit to the base of a three-loop unit, as shown, to form a kind of inverted triangle.

5 Cut three 8-in. (20-cm) lengths of 0.5 mm nylon filament. Thread a silver crimp bead onto the first length. Feed the filament through the first loop of one three-loop unit and double the nylon back onto itself, through the crimp bead, to form a small loop. Squeeze the crimp bead with your chain-nose pliers to secure.

6 Thread the nylon filament with eight amethyst chips, pushing them right up against the crimp bead, and then thread on another crimp bead and squeeze it with your chain-nose pliers to secure. Leave a gap of about ½ in. (1 cm), then secure another crimp bead on the filament. Thread on eight more chips and another crimp bead, as before. Repeat until the filament is full, placing a crimp bead at the start and end of each block of eight chips in order to keep them separate.

7 Attach the second length of filament to the central loop of the same three-loop unit, then fill it with chips, as in step 6—but this time, make blocks of five amethyst chips. Attach the third length of filament to the remaining loop of the three-loop unit, then fill it with blocks of three amethyst chips. Attach the other ends of the three lengths of filament to the corresponding loops on the second silver unit.

8 To make the chain links, cut 16 2-in. (5-cm) lengths of 20-gauge (0.8 mm) silver wire. Using your round-nose pliers, curl a circle at one end of each wire. Curl another circle at the other end of the wire, facing in toward the first. Hold the circles firmly in your flat-nose pliers and spiral them in toward each other until they meet in the center of the wire.

9 Gently hammer the units on a steel stake to work harden them (see page 185).

10 Make 18 jump rings. Starting and ending with a jump ring, connect eight units together to form one side of the chain. Repeat to form the second side.

11 Now attach the chains to the amethyst centerpiece. Make another four jump rings. Link one jump ring into each loop of a two-loop unit, then connect them both to the jump ring at the end of each section of chain.

12 Make a fish-hook clasp and eye (see pages 184 and 186). Attach the clasp to one section of chain and the eye to the other.

VARIATION:
Positive Energy

I call this a "Positive Energy" necklace, as it combines the energies of different semi-precious stones in one piece. The stones are crimped onto black nylon filament.

Bead Spray Brooch

This delicate brooch looks wonderful pinned to a jacket lapel, or worn on a smart, single-color sweater or dress. You can choose any colored beads that blend together or create something that is quite classic, perhaps using a traditional combination of pearl beads with gold wire.

YOU WILL NEED

- 26-gauge (0.4 mm) wire
- 20-gauge (0.8 mm) wire
- Beads
- Masking tape
- Superglue (optional)
- Wire cutters
- Round-nose pliers
- Ready-made brooch fitting

OPPOSITE *This delightful little spray of bead "flowers" could not be simpler to make—the perfect project for the novice jewelry maker!*

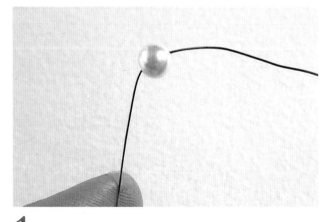

1 Cut 4–5-in. (10–12.5-cm) lengths of 26-gauge (0.4 mm) wire. Thread a bead or beads onto the center of the wires, then fold the wires down on each side.

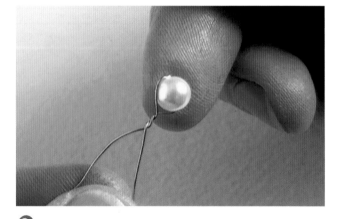

2 Bring both wires together around the bead and twist, securing the bead at the end.

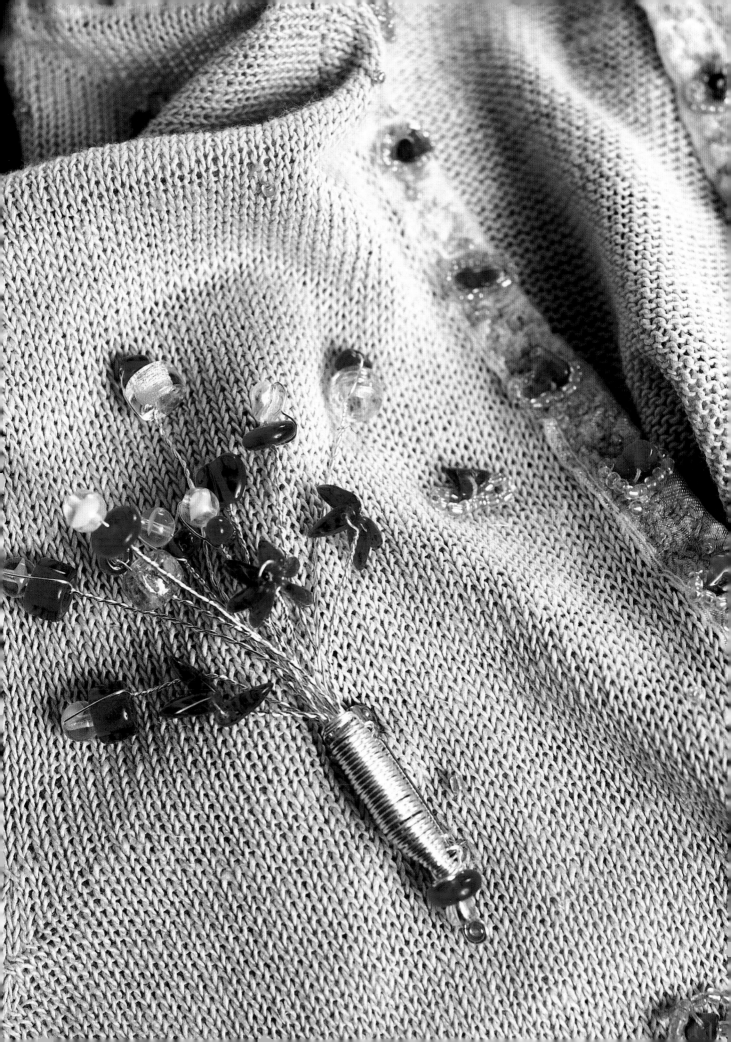

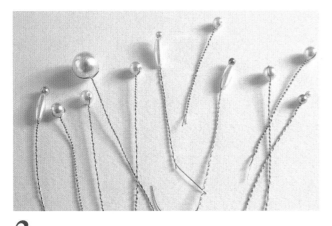

3 Continue twisting all the beads (about eight to ten strands) onto the 26-gauge (0.4 mm) wire in this way until you have a pleasing combination or bouquet.

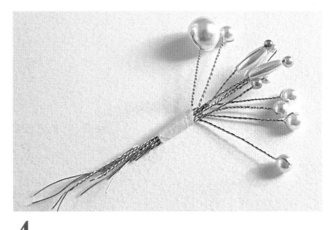

4 Place the wire stems together in a bunch with the heads at an even height, then bind the stems together with masking tape to secure them in position.

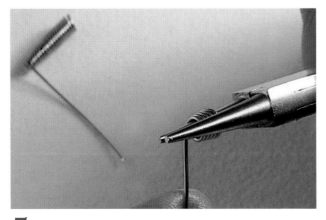

5 Using 20-gauge (0.8 mm) wire, form a tube or coil by binding the wire around the shaft of your round-nose pliers or a cylindrical object. Leave at least 1 in. (2.5 cm) of wire extending from the coil.

6 Place the stems of your bead bouquet into this coiled tube, hiding the masking tape, and secure around the bunched wires, by squeezing the top rung of the coil tightly around the stems.

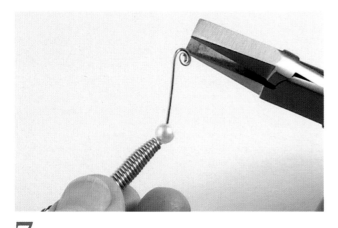

7 Thread an extra bead onto the extended wire of the coil and turn the end into a spiral, to prevent the bead sliding off. (If you wish, dab a little superglue around the 20-gauge (0.8 mm) coil, to ensure the stems of the wired beads are firmly secured within the tube.)

8 Using 26-gauge (0.4 mm) wire directly from the spool, bind the brooch finding securely to the back of the bouquet stems.

9 Spend a little time gently adjusting the angles of the sprays of beads so that they form an attractive arrangement. To avoid the brooch catching on other clothing, it is best to keep the arrangement fairly flat, so that it lies close to your body.

Squiggle Ring

Squiggles of wire, achieved simply by bending the wire around your pliers, make up the top of this modern-looking ring. The irregular sizes and angles of the bends are all part of the design's charm, so don't worry about making it look symmetrical! The ring is very quick to make, as it's all formed from one continuous piece of wire. You can use colored or plated wire, sterling silver or gold, for this project. Practice with copper wire, just to build up your confidence; once you've mastered the technique, you'll be all set to make one in 14-carat gold!

YOU WILL NEED

- 12–14 in. (30–35 cm) 20-gauge (0.8 mm) wire
- 1 decorative 4 mm bead
- Round- and flat-nose pliers
- Wire cutters
- Mandrel or dowel

OPPOSITE *Add a variety of different beads to this ring to really make it stand out.*

VARIATION:
Colored Squiggles

Colored wire makes a fun and funky alternative to the gold wire shown in the demonstration. Choose a focal bead that stands out well, such as a clear bead against jet black wire, or a metallic bead against bright red.

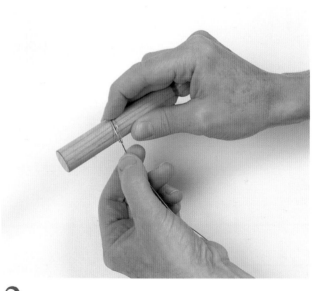

1 Cut a 12–14-in. (30–35-cm) length of 20-gauge (0.8 mm) wire.

2 Wrap the wire a couple of times tightly around a mandrel, or a dowel slightly smaller in diameter than you want the finished ring, to shape the shank.

3 Wrap the cut end of the wire around the shank two or three times, leaving at least 5–6 in. (12–15 cm) of wire extending. Use your flat-nose pliers to press the wire tightly against the shank and secure the wire.

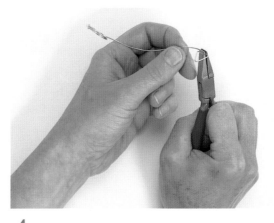

4 Hold the end of the extended wire with your flat-nose pliers and bend it in small, random angles.

5 Increase the size of the bends in the wire as you get closer to the shank of the ring.

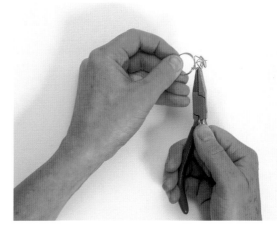

6 Keep bending the wire in angular folds until it sits directly against the ring shank.

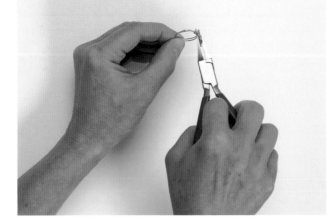

7 Flatten the bent wire against the ring shank with your flat-nose pliers and spend a little time rearranging it into a shape that you like by twisting the wire around with your pliers to expose the layers underneath.

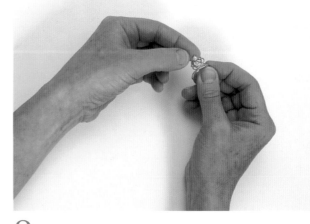

8 Using the very tips of your round-nose pliers, pull the central end wire out of the squiggle. Then thread a small focal bead onto it.

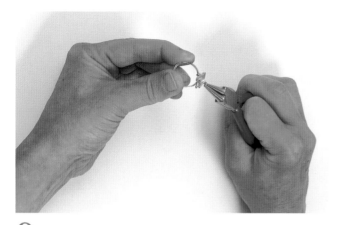

9 To secure the bead, make a small hook at the end of the wire using the tips of your round-nose pliers.

10 Squash the hook flat with the ends of your flat-nose pliers to create a knob of wire, which will prevent the bead from slipping off. Spend a little extra time rearranging the front of the ring until you are satisfied with the centerpiece.

VARIATION:
Beadless Squiggles

You can also make squiggle rings entirely from wire, without any focal bead in the center. To do this, form the ring shank, as described in steps 1 through 3, and then form a spiral (see page 182) or wiggly shape for the top of the ring. Complete the ring by bending the wire at random angles until it sits snugly against the ring shank.

Celtic Cross

A silver cross filled with large beads makes a dramatic statement when worn with a simple black sweater. This design is a simplified, modern-day interpretation of a traditional Celtic-style cross. Celtic crosses differ from the later Christian crosses, which have a longer central stem; it is believed that they were designed symmetrically to fit into a circle (the symbol of the cycle of life). My design is suspended from a hand-made chain of S-shaped units threaded with tiny seed beads, but you could use a ready-made chain if you prefer.

YOU WILL NEED

- 20-gauge (0.8 mm) silver wire
- 18-gauge (1 mm) silver wire
- Selection of 2–4 mm green and transparent beads
- 1 x 8 mm green focal bead
- 24 x size 8/0 green seed beads
- Round- and flat-nose pliers
- Wire cutters
- Jig and 13 small pegs
- Jig pattern on page 190
- Hammer and steel stake

OPPOSITE *This elegant cross has a centerpiece of green faceted beads, suspended from a hand-made S-link chain.*

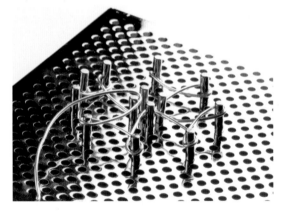

1 Cut a 33-cm (13-in.) length of 18-gauge (1 mm) silver wire. Following the pattern on page 190, place the pegs in your jig. Using your round-nose pliers, form a loop at one end of the wire and pull it tightly around the first peg. Now loop the wire around the remaining pegs, following the pattern. Snip off any excess wire.

2 Remove the wire motif from the pegs and gently "stroke" hammer the unit on a steel stake (see page 185) to work harden it.

3 Using your flat-nose pliers, turn the top two links through 90° so that they face each other.

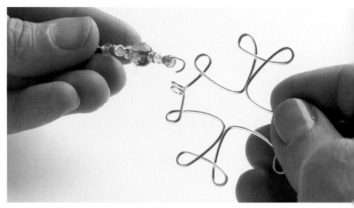

4 Lay the beads down the center of the cross to work out the arrangement. Cut a piece of 20-gauge (0.8 mm) silver wire about 1½ in. (4 cm) longer than the cross. Using your round-nose pliers, form a link at one end (see page 180) and thread on the beads. Using your flat-nose pliers, form a small, tight spiral at the other end of the wire (see page 182).

5 Thread the link through the top two loops of the cross and close it with your flat-nose pliers.

6 Bend the spiral over the base of the cross and press firmly with your fingers to hold it in place.

7 To make a 16-in. (40-cm) chain, cut 24 1-in. (2.5-cm) lengths of 20-gauge (0.8 mm) silver wire. Using your round-nose pliers, form a complete circle at one end of each wire and thread on one size 8/0 green seed bead. Using your round-nose pliers, form another complete circle at the other end of each wire, trapping the green bead in between the two circles.

8 Make 26 jump rings (see page 182) from 20-gauge (0.8 mm) silver wire. Starting and ending with a jump ring, connect 12 S-shaped units together. Repeat, using the remaining jump rings and S-shaped units.

VARIATION:
Plaited Choker

For a more casual effect, make the cross using different colors of beads and suspend it from a plaited cord choker in matching colors or from a bail, as in the Wrapped Stone Pendant on page 58.

9 Connect one end of each chain to the top link of the cross.

10 To complete the necklace, make a spiral clasp from 20-gauge (0.8 mm) wire and attach it to the ends of the chains.

Art Deco Necklace

With its gently curving loops and hanging bead, this elegant necklace was inspired by the Art Deco period of the early 20th century. You can easily improvise on this design by hanging it upside down or by reducing or enlarging the size of the loops.

OPPOSITE Experiment with different colors to create the perfect necklace and earrings to match a Twenties-inspired outfit.

YOU WILL NEED

- 20-gauge (0.8 mm) wire
- Beads
- Ready-made chain
- Wire cutters
- Round-nose pliers
- Cylindrical dowel
- Hammer and steel block

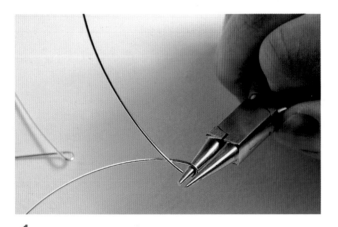

1 Cut two 6-in. (15-cm) lengths of 20-gauge (0.8 mm) wire. Find the center of each wire with your round-nose pliers and cross the wires over.

2 Curl the wires loosely around a cylindrical dowel or thick pen shaft to create a large loop that faces away from the center and crosses over the outer frame.

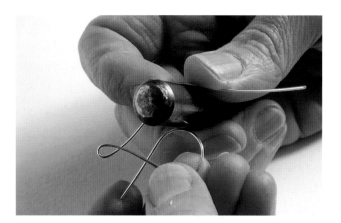

3 Using the dowel, form a similar circular loop on the other side of the frame, as in step 2. The two loops should face away from each other.

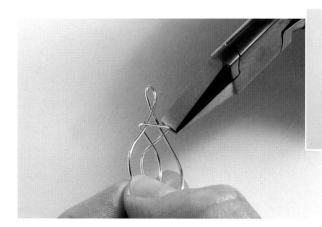

4 Secure the projecting ends of the wire around the main framework of the piece by wrapping it near the top central link.

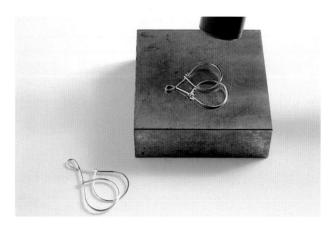

5 Gently hammer the pieces on a steel block to straighten and flatten them. Be careful not to hammer on any crossed-over wires as this will weaken them.

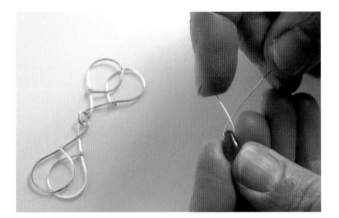

6 When you have created two identical units, connect them together with jump rings (see page 182), using your flat-nose pliers.

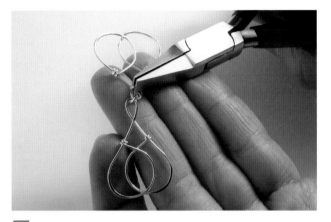

7 Thread a small bead with wire to form the center of your necklace.

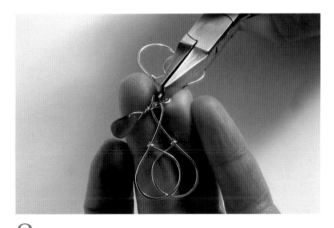

8 Connect this bead to the center of the units, using flat-nose pliers. Ensure that the link is securely closed.

9 To make the chain, thread your chosen beads onto wires (see page 180).

10 Using round-nose pliers, form links on each side of your threaded beads.

11 Using wire cutters, cut the ready-made chain in short, equal lengths.

12 Link the threaded beads onto the chain at regular intervals, using flat-nose pliers.

13 Link the chain to your central unit, making sure the sides are symmetrical. Add a clasp of your choice, made from the same wire as the rest of the necklace (see pages 184–9).

Art Deco Earrings

These earrings should be made slightly smaller than the necklace centerpiece by using 5-in. (12.5-cm) lengths of 20-gauge (0.8 mm) wire. Follow steps 1 to 5 of the necklace, then continue as shown below.

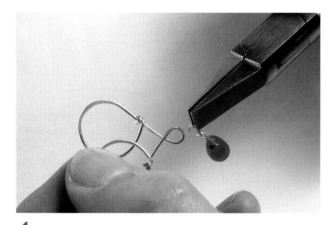

1 Thread a bead onto wire and suspend this from the looped end of the unit.

2 Connect ear wires to the other end. Repeat to make the second earring.

VARIATION:
Art Nouveau Earrings

This variation is created in a similar way to the Art Deco design on page 26, but is more elaborate. The chain is made with threaded beads, interspersed with beaded S-links. The centerpiece has a tasseled pendant, and the earrings have been suspended in the opposite direction to the Art Deco earrings, shown above.

Falling Leaves Necklace

Beaded leaves in autumnal shades of copper and bronze form the centerpiece of this stylish necklace. If this particular design is too elaborate for your tastes, simplify it by using just three leaf units on a ready-made chain. The wire leaves can be attached to many other things, too. Why not use them as decorations for greetings cards and scrapbook layouts, or as gift tags?

YOU WILL NEED

- Approx. 75 size 11/0 gold-colored seed beads
- Six 6 mm copper-colored beads
- One oblong focal bead, about 20 mm long
- Eight 8 mm brown and two 10 mm light-brown faceted beads
- 20- and 26-gauge (0.8 mm and 0.4 mm) copper wire
- Round- and flat-nose pliers
- Wire cutters
- Hammer and steel block

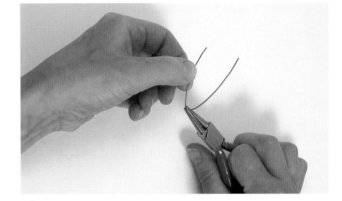

1 Decide how long you want the leaves to be and cut just over double that amount of 20-gauge (0.8mm) copper wire for each one. Bend the wire in two, just past the halfway point, so that one section is slightly longer than the other.

2 Using your flat-nose pliers, wrap the longer wire tightly around the shorter wire two or three times. Snip off any excess, leaving the shorter wire extending by about ½ in. (1 cm).

VARIATION:
Leaf Earrings

Follow steps 1 through 8 to make two identical leaves. Make two jump rings and then suspend the leaves from ready-made ear wires.

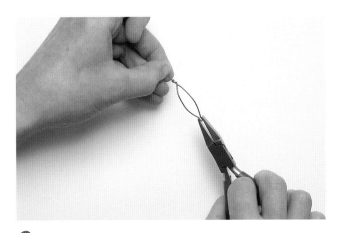

3 At the other end of the leaf, squeeze the wires together with your flat-nose pliers, leaving a narrow channel between them.

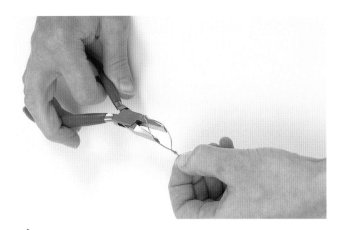

4 Place your flat-nose pliers in the center of the leaf and pry the wires apart by opening the pliers. Using your pliers, adjust the piece into a leaf shape.

5 Hammer the wire frame on your steel block to work harden it, avoiding the wrapped end (see page 185).

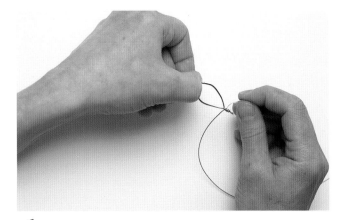

6 Curl the extending wire into a link (see page 180). Wrap 26-gauge (0.4 mm) wire around the top of the leaf under the link. Make three more leaves in the same way.

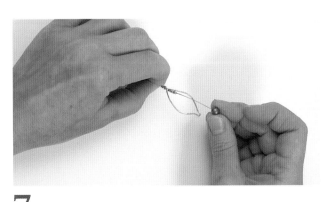

7 Pull this narrow wire straight down the center of the leaf shape and cut it off from the spool, leaving at least ½ in. (1 cm) extending. Thread gold seed beads onto this wire all the way up to the tip of the leaf, with one 6-mm copper bead in the center as a focal bead.

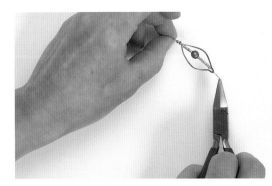

8 Using your flat-nose pliers, wrap any excess wire around the end tip of the leaf a couple of times to secure it.

9 Make two small leaves, using 2½ in. (7 cm) of 20-gauge (0.8 mm) wire. Thread them with 6–8 seed beads. Make a large leaf from 6 in. (15 cm) of wire. Thread the oblong focal bead at the center and one 6-mm copper bead and two seed beads on either side.

10 Make a beaded chain by threading four 8 mm faceted brown beads, linked together with jump rings, followed by two 10-mm lighter brown beads and four more 8 mm beads.

11 Cut twelve 1-in. (2.5-cm) pieces of 20-gauge (0.8 mm) copper wire. Curl half of each piece around your round-nose pliers, then turn the wire over and curl the remainder in the opposite direction to make an S-shape.

12 Connect the S-shapes together with jump rings to make two chains of six S-shapes. Attach one to each side of the beaded chain. Suspend the large leaf from the jump ring between the largest two beads of the beaded chain, with two medium leaves and one small leaf on either side of it. Make a clasp (see pages 184–9).

VARIATION:
Corded Leaf Choker

For a simple, more casual design, make one large leaf and suspend it from a cord. To make the fastener at the end of the choker, make two coils of wire that fit the diameter of the cord. Cut the coil off the wire spool, leaving 1 in. (2.5 cm) of wire extending, and curl the ends into links. Slide the coils onto the ends of the cord and secure by squeezing the last rung of the coil tightly against the cord with your flat-nose pliers. (You can apply a little adhesive for added security!) Attach a fish-hook clasp (see page 184) to the links at the ends of the coils.

Double Spiral Necklace

Spirals are one of the simplest and most satisfying of shapes to make from wire and I use them a lot in my designs. It's amazing how different they can look, depending on whether the spirals are open or closed and on what thickness of wire you use. Each unit in this necklace is made from one piece of doubled-over wire, providing a very solid, metallic effect. I used two contrasting colors of wire for added impact.

YOU WILL NEED

- ✂ 20-gauge (0.8 mm) copper wire
- ✂ 20-gauge (0.8 mm) silver wire
- ✂ Round- and flat-nose pliers
- ✂ Wire cutters

1 Cut six 6-in. (15-cm) lengths of 20-gauge (0.8 mm) silver wire and 12 of copper. Bend each length in half by placing the tips of your round-nose pliers in the center and pulling and straightening the wire on each side until it runs straight and parallel.

2 Using your flat-nose pliers, squeeze the doubled wires together so that they run parallel to each other.

3 Using the tips of your round-nose pliers, curl the doubled end into a hook, making sure that the wires remain parallel to one another and do not overlap.

OPPOSITE *The double-spiral units can be linked into attractive necklace chains using any colored wire combinations. For a lighter effect, intersperse beads or coiled wire spacers between the spirals (top).*

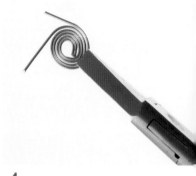

LEFT *Two silver jump rings connect the copper and silver spiral units together and help to balance the design.*

4 Using your flat-nose pliers, curl the doubled wires into a tight spiral until you are left with about ½ in. (1 cm) of wire.

5 Separate the projecting wires and, using your round-nose pliers, curl the bottom wire into a link (see page 180).

6 Curl the top projecting wire into another link, curling it around your round-nose pliers until it sits opposite the first link. Cut off any excess wire.

7 Make 34 jump rings from 20-gauge (0.8 mm) silver wire (see page 182). Placing two jump rings between each unit, connect the spirals together, adding one silver spiral after every two copper.

8 To complete the necklace, make a spiral clasp using 20-gauge (0.8 mm) silver wire.

BELOW *This close-up photograph shows the hammered spiral clasp, which provides a tough, but decorative, finishing touch.*

Beaded Scarf Slide

Subtle and understated, this stylish little beaded slide is an elegant way of holding a scarf in place. Choose a focal bead and wire color that tone in with the colors in the scarf fabric, so that the slide does not detract from the scarf. Do, however, make sure that the central hole in your focal bead is big enough to be threaded with a doubled length of 20-gauge (0.8 mm) wire.

YOU WILL NEED

- 16-gauge (1.2 mm), 20-gauge (0.8 mm), and 26-gauge (0.4 mm) silver wire
- 1 x 8 mm focal bead
- Round- and flat-nose pliers
- Wire cutters
- Hammer and steel stake

1 Cut two 5-in. (12.5-cm) lengths of 16-gauge (1.2 mm) silver wire. Using your fingers, twist one wire around the other two or three times about ½ in. (1 cm) from the end. Cut off one of the short ends of wire and flatten the end against the stem with your flat-nose pliers.

2 Form the other short end of wire into a tiny closed spiral (see page 182). Bend the spiral over the wire and, using your flat-nose pliers, squeeze it flat against the wrapped wire to conceal it.

OPPOSITE *Feed the ends of the scarf under the slanted central bar, so that the focal bead remains visible.*

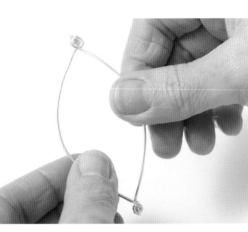

3 Repeat steps 1 and 2 to secure the other side. Using your fingers, gently pull the sides of the wire frame apart to create an elongated oval shape.

4 Using a hammer on a steel stake, gently stroke hammer the outer frame to work harden it (see page 185), avoiding the spirals.

6 The spirals should end just beyond the widest part of the frame; keep checking as you work, to make sure that they're not too big.

5 Cut two 4-in. (10-cm) lengths of 20-gauge (0.8 mm) silver wire, hold them both together in your hand, and thread your focal bead onto the center. At each end of each wire, make a small closed spiral about ¼ in. (5 mm) in diameter, spiraling outward in opposite directions.

Check that your focal bead can be threaded with doubled 20-gauge (0.8 mm) wire.

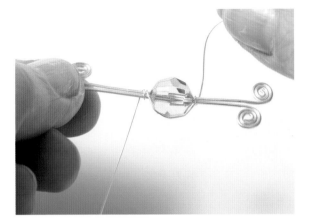

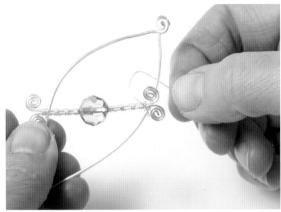

7 Cut a 10–12-in. (20–25-cm) length of 26-gauge (0.4 mm) silver wire. Find the center and wrap it two or three times around the doubled wires, just next to the bead. Take the wire over the back of the bead, then continue wrapping it around the doubled wires in both directions, working right up to the small spirals.

8 Use the ends of the binding wire to attach the beaded bar across the widest point of the frame, angling it slightly on the diagonal.

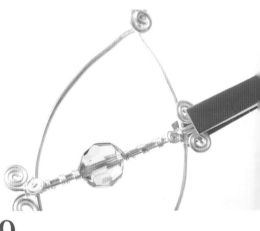

9 When you've got about ½ in. (1 cm) of binding wire left on each side, form it into tiny spirals. Using your flat-nose pliers, flatten them against the bar as extra decoration.

VARIATION:
Beaded Beauty

For a more flamboyant effect, omit steps 7 and 8, fill the cross bar with beads, and wrap the outer frame in colored wire.

Spiral Choker

Vibrant turquoise and green wires, reminiscent of peacock feathers, are twisted together to form the ring of this choker, with spirals of the same colors creating the centerpiece. Use a combination of tight and more open spirals to give the piece a sense of airiness.

For a more classic look, try combining gold and silver wires. Increase or reduce the amount of wire that you spiral to suit your own taste. This is one of those designs that evolves and grows as you create it; it can never look the same way twice!

YOU WILL NEED

- Three tones of 24-gauge (0.6mm) wire, approx. 60 in. (150 cm) of each
- Masking tape
- Round- and flat-nose pliers
- Wire cutters
- Hand drill
- Table vise
- Hammer and steel block

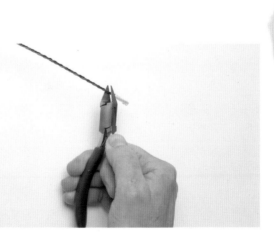

1 Cut three 20-in. (50-cm) lengths of 24-gauge (0.6mm) wire, one from each color of wire. Bind the ends together with masking tape. Place one taped end in the table vise and the other in the chuck of the hand drill. Slowly turn the drill handle, keeping all wires taut. Once all the wires have twisted evenly, remove from the drill and vise and cut off the taped ends.

OPPOSITE *This choker is made from toning shades of blue and green, which gives it a lovely color harmony.*

45

2 Unravel 1½ in. (4 cm) at one end of the twist and separate the wires. Wrap two of the three wires around the twisted stem to secure. Snip off any spiky ends.

3 Using your round-nose pliers, curl the end of the remaining wire into a small loop.

4 Create a second, much larger, loop by curling the wire in the opposite direction, just under the first circle, to complete the fish-hook fastener.

5 Hammer the end of the fish hook to flatten and work harden it—but do not hammer any of the wrapped wires or they will become weak and brittle.

6 To form the eye of the fastener, unravel the wires on the opposite end of the twist, as in step 2, and separate them out. Wrap two of the wires around the stem of the twist, until you are left with just one wire protruding. Bend this wire at right angles and then form a loop around your round-nose pliers, with the end overlapping the stem. Secure by wrapping it around the stem a couple of times. Cut off any excess. Hammer the end of the loop, as in step 5, to work harden it.

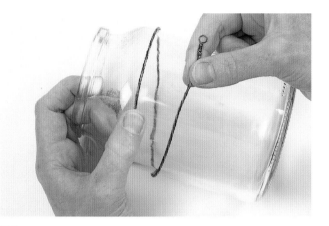

7 To create the circular shape of the choker, find a cylindrical object about 4 in. (10 cm) in diameter (such as a bottle or cookie jar) and wrap the twisted wires around it tightly, overlapping the ends.

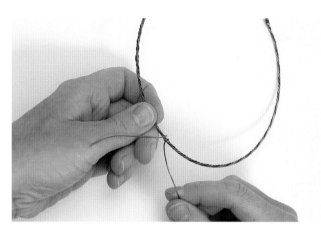

8 Cut 10–15 pieces of 24-gauge (0.6 mm) colored wire, 6–8 in. (15–20 cm) in length and the same number of pieces from each of your three colors of wire. Wrap the center of the first wire around the center of the choker frame, leaving both ends sticking out.

9 Continue until you have used up all the wires, making sure that they are centered on the front of the choker ring.

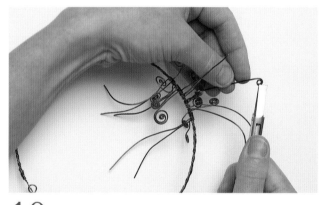

10 Spiral the ends of the wires (see page 182), leaving a small gap between the spirals and the choker frame. Make both open and closed spirals.

11 Spend a little time arranging the centerpiece, twisting the spirals together and over each other with your fingers to create a solid front. You can add more spirals if you want a fuller effect.

BEAUTIFUL JEWELRY:

Working with Beads

Packed with beads in every shape, size, and color of the rainbow, a good bead store is like an Aladdin's Cave for jewelry makers! This chapter demonstrates some of the many ways of using beads, from the eye-catching use of a single feature bead, as in the Tassel Clip and Simple Bead Ring (pages 74 and 78), through threading several beads onto a wire, as in the Beaded Bangle on page 70, to more elaborate combinations such as the cluster of beads in the Ice Crystal Necklace (page 50). You will also learn how to make your very own "charms," as in the Bead Charm Necklace (page 62), how to incorporate items that do not have a drilled hole into pieces of jewelry (Wrapped Stone Pendant, page 58), how to make beaded tendrils (Twinkly Hair Grip, page 66), and how to connect "bars" of wire threaded with beads into a chain bracelet (Sea-blue Bracelet, page 54).

Dressed to Impress

Looking for a really bold piece of jewelry to set off a special outfit or to reflect your own flamboyant personality? This chapter is packed full of dramatic designs that have real visual impact. From chunky bangles and brilliantly colored bracelets to outsized rings, these are jewelry pieces for women who want to make a definite style statement. If you enjoy being the center of attention, read on!

Ice Crystal Necklace

Frost and ice glistening in the winter sunshine were the inspiration for this necklace, which is made up of clear glass beads and crystals. As it is so neutral in coloring, it can be worn with any outfit and will suit both young and old. Matching earrings can be made using a variety of threaded beads and flattened wire "feathers" suspended from ear wires.

I used a ready-made chain, although you could make your own. Whichever you choose, check that the links are large enough to take the 20-gauge (0.8 mm) wire used to thread the beads.

OPPOSITE *Clear glass and silver "feathers" give this necklace a wonderfully frosty, wintry feel.*

YOU WILL NEED

- 24 clear glass beads in varying shapes, ranging in size from 3 mm to 10 mm
- 20-gauge (0.8 mm) silver wire
- 17 in. (42.5 cm) ready-made chain
- Round- and flat-nose pliers
- Wire cutters
- Hammer and steel block

1 Thread your beads with wire, forming a head pin at one end and a link at the other (see pages 180–1).

2 As an alternative to a head pin, you could spiral the end of the wire (see page 182).

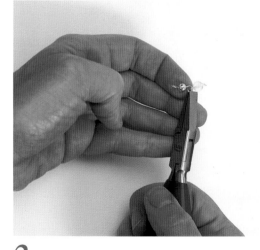

3 If you are using very small beads, link some together in a chain-like formation.

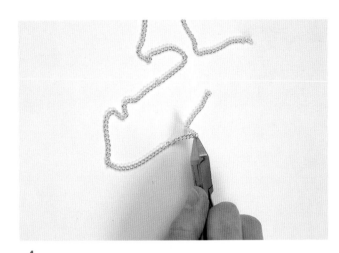

4 Cut a 17-in. (42.5-cm) length of ready-made chain and snip 2 in. (5 cm) off the end.

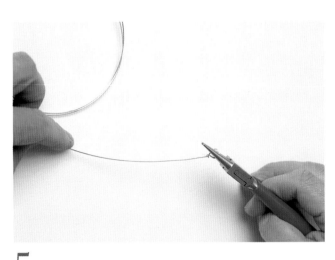

5 Curl a length of wire around your round-nose pliers to make a loop, and wrap the excess around itself, as you would when making the eye of a clasp. Leave enough of the wire stem free to add on a bead.

6 Thread a clear bead onto the end of this wire and curl the other end into a link (see page 180).

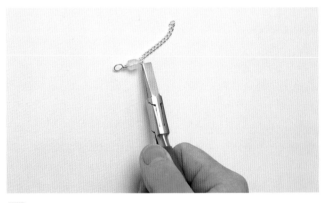

7 Attach the link to one end of the 2-in. (5-cm) piece of chain and close with flat-nose pliers to secure.

8 Make jump rings (see page 182) and connect your threaded beads to the large loop in the 2-in. (5-cm) chain, starting with smaller beads at one end, increasing in size as you near the center, and finishing with smaller beads at the other end of the chain.

9 Cut 4–6 pieces of wire 1–1½ in. (2.5–4 cm) in length. Curl one end into a link with your round-nose pliers (see page 180), threading with beads if desired. Gently hammer the other end on a steel block until the wire spreads into a "feather" shape.

10 Link these wire "feathers" in between the beads to add sparkle to your icy cascade.

11 Thread the cascade of beads onto the 15-in. (37.5 cm) chain and connect a clasp to the ends.

VARIATION:
Green Bead Cascade

These bead bunches, or cascades, can be made from any range of assorted beads. In fact, it's a great way of using up odd beads from old, broken necklaces, giving them a new lease on life! This green cascade has hand-made silver "hieroglyphs" between the beads for added decoration.

Sea-blue Bracelet

With rows of turquoise chip stones evoking the azure blue of a tropical sea, this chunky bracelet would look fabulous worn with a simple white T-shirt. A ready-made chain forms the basis of the bracelet, so it's relatively quick to make. You will, however, need to cut a length of chain in half and then reconnect the ends with jump rings, rather than use a single length of chain, in order to form the tapered ends. Also, make sure that the links of your chain are wide enough to thread with 20-gauge (0.8 mm) wire.

YOU WILL NEED

- ✿ Turquoise chips
- ✿ 10–12-in. (25–30-cm) length of ready-made silver chain
- ✿ 20-gauge (0.8 mm) silver wire
- ✿ Round- and flat-nose pliers
- ✿ Wire cutters

OPPOSITE *The semi-precious turquoise chip stone that I used in this bracelet is purported to promote spiritual attunement and well-being.*

1 Cut two 5–6-in. (12.5–15-cm) lengths of ready-made chain. Make a jump ring from 20-gauge (0.8 mm) silver wire (see page 182) and thread it through one end of each section of chain to join them together.

2 Thread two turquoise chips onto the end of a spool of 20-gauge (0.8 mm) silver wire. Leave about ½ in. (1 cm) protruding on each side of the beads and cut the wire off the spool.

3 Take the chips off the wire. Form a small spiraled head pin at one end of the wire (see page 181). Straighten the other end of the wire if necessary.

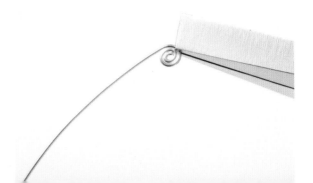

4 Count three chain links down from the jump ring on one side of the chain and slide the pin into the link from the outside. Rethread the pin with the two turquoise chips and slide it through the third link on the opposite side of the chain.

5 Form a spiraled head pin on the other side to hold the chips in place.

VARIATION:
Tiny Beads

The bracelet and earrings shown here are made using bugle and seed beads, creating a more open and delicate effect.

6 Repeat steps 2–5 along the length of the bracelet, increasing the chips on each unit to three, and then four or five. Decrease the number of chips at the end of the bracelet. Leave three links of the chain between each beaded unit.

Birthstone Chart

Month and zodiac sign	Semi-precious stone	Color
JANUARY 1–19 Jan. (Capricorn) 20–31 Jan. (Aquarius)	Garnet	Deep red/burgundy
FEBRUARY 1–18 Feb. (Aquarius) 19–28 Feb. (Pisces)	Amethyst	Purple
MARCH 1–20 March (Pisces) 21–31 March (Aries)	Aquamarine	Pale blue
APRIL 1–19 April (Aries) 20–30 April (Taurus)	Diamond	Clear/colorless clear crystal
MAY 1–20 May (Taurus) 21–31 May (Gemini)	Emerald	Green
JUNE 1–21 June (Gemini) 22–30 June (Cancer)	Pearl	Cream
JULY 1–22 July (Cancer) 23–31 July (Leo)	Ruby	Bright red
AUGUST 1–22 August (Leo) 23–31 August (Virgo)	Peridot	Pale green
SEPTEMBER 1–22 Sept. (Virgo) 23–30 Sept. (Libra)	Sapphire	Pale blue
OCTOBER 1–23 Oct. (Libra) 24–31 Oct. (Scorpio)	Opal	Variegated/ multi-colored
NOVEMBER 1–21 Nov. (Scorpio) 22–30 Nov. (Sagittarius)	Topaz	Yellow
DECEMBER 1–21 Dec. (Sagittarius) 22–31 Dec. (Capricorn)	Turquoise	Bright blue

7 When the bracelet is full, join the two chains by attaching a jump ring to the chain ends. Position the ring three chain links from the last beaded unit, as shown.

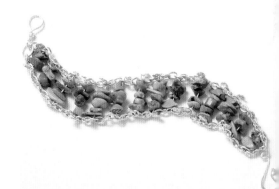

8 Make a fish-hook clasp and eye (see pages 184 and 186) and connect them to the jump rings at each end of the bracelet.

Wrapped Stone Pendant

YOU WILL NEED

- Polished stone 1¼–1½ in. (3–4 cm) in length
- 20-gauge (0.8 mm) silver wire
- 16-in. (40-cm) length of 1 mm black cotton cord
- Round- and flat-nose pliers
- Wire cutters

I used a polished stone for this pendant, but for a more natural look you could substitute a pebble worn smooth by the sea. The technique of wrapping a stone in wire can be used for anything that does not have a drilled hole, from shells to fragments of china—the perfect way of creating a lasting souvenir of a special trip or of preserving a favorite piece of crockery. Just make sure that the item you choose has no jagged edges that could scratch or cut the wearer.

OPPOSITE *Stones of all shapes and sizes can be lightly wrapped in wire to create striking centerpieces.*

1 Cut a length of 20-gauge (0.8 mm) silver wire approximately four times the length of the stone. Curl one end into an open spiral (see page 182).

2 Hold the spiral at the top of the stone, flat against the back, and pull the wire down to the base of the stone.

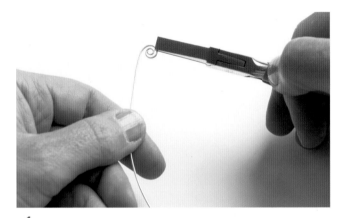

3 Wrap the wire around the front and middle of the stone a couple of times and then bring it around to the top of the front of the stone.

ABOVE *Here you can see an alternative version of the end clasp, which has a wire heart decoration. A spiral or threaded bead would look equally attractive.*

4 Using your fingers, uncoil the spiral at the back of the stone.

5 Wrap the cut end of the wire around the stem to secure. Cut off any excess and neaten the ends (see page 187).

6 Using your round-nose pliers, form a link at the end of the protruding wire (see page 180). Cut off any excess wire and neaten the ends.

7 To form the top bail of the pendant, cut a 4¾-in. (12-cm) length of 20-gauge (0.8 mm) silver wire and fold it in half, squeezing the ends together so that the doubled wires run parallel to each other.

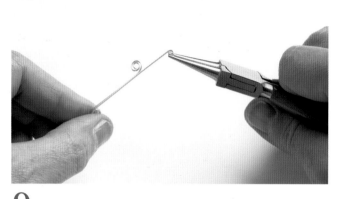

8 Using the ends of your round-nose pliers, curl the doubled-up end of wire into a loop.

9 Holding the loop in your left hand, curl a spiral at each loose end of the wire, curling the spirals outward in opposite directions.

10 Place the widest part of your round-nose pliers around the wires just past the loop and bend the wires down to form a hook.

11 Attach the link at the top of the wrapped stone into the doubled link on the bail.

12 Thread a length of jewelry cord through the center of the bail. Make sure that the spirals are pressed firmly against the front. Make a coiled fish-hook clasp and fastener for the cord (see page 189).

Bead Charm Necklace

If you're new to making wire jewelry, this is a great piece to start with as it gives you the chance to practice many different ways of threading beads and connecting different elements together. Before you begin, spend time looking at the colors and shapes of your beads and other decorations to ensure that they work well together. I put in lots of charms, because I like the richness of having them packed closely together, but a few randomly scattered beads can look just as effective.

YOU WILL NEED

- ❧ Selection of beads in different shapes and sizes, ranging from 4 to 12 mm
- ❧ 4–6 coin findings
- ❧ Approx. 6 ft (2 m) 20-gauge (0.8 mm) gold wire
- ❧ Approx. 16 in. (40 cm) ready-made chain
- ❧ Round- and flat-nose pliers
- ❧ Wire cutters
- ❧ Hammer and steel block

OPPOSITE *The rich red, orange, and gold color scheme gives this necklace a really opulent feel.*

1 First, make up the individual charms. One option is to thread your beads onto wires, forming links at one end and head pins or spirals at the other (see pages 181–2).

2 If you have lots of tiny beads, you can link two or more together in short chains.

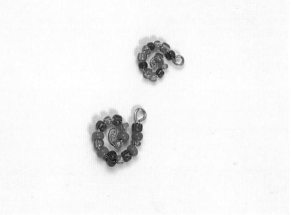

3 For added color, you can make spirals of wire and thread them with seed beads.

4 Cut 1-in. (2-5-cm) lengths of wire. Form a link at one end and hammer the other end on a steel block, so that it flattens and spreads into a feather shape.

5 You can also form curly wiggles of wire, to your own designs.

6 Select a ready-made chain that can be threaded with 20-gauge (0.8-mm) jump rings, cut a 7-in. (18-cm) length, and make a beaded link to attach to each end. Work out the order that you want the charms to go in.

VARIATION:
Bead Charm Bracelet and Earrings

Create a bracelet in the same way as the necklace, adding a clasp at the end of step 7 and omitting step 8. For bold, matching earrings, make two bead bunches and attach them to ready-made ear wires.

7 Make jump rings (see page 182) and attach the charms to the chain.

8 Connect enough ready-made chain on each side of the charm chain to extend the necklace to the length you want. Make a clasp (see pages 184–9) and attach to each end of the necklace.

VARIATION:
Bold and Gold

Changing the color scheme creates a very different mood: in the jade and gold color scheme (bottom), caged glass beads are interspersed with gold spirals and twists. Alternatively, gold-colored coins (such as the ones used in the Belly Dancer's Bracelet on page 172), semiprecious chip beads, and gold-wire "hieroglyphic" symbols make a striking decoration (top).

Twinkly Hair Grip

Encrusted with sparkling pearl, crystal, and gold bugle beads, this highly decorative hair grip is guaranteed to twinkle and shine at any party gathering! It would also make a wonderful bridal accessory and could be pinned at the back of the head to hide the comb on the bride's veil. If this color scheme is a little too sedate for your tastes, or you're making the hair grip for a little girl rather than an adult, use brightly colored beads and attach the hair grip to the side of a hairband.

YOU WILL NEED

- 26-gauge (0.4 mm) and 20-gauge (0.8 mm) gold wire
- Pearl, gold bugle, and crystal beads, 2–8 mm in diameter
- 1 x 1 cm pearl feature bead
- Masking tape
- Nylon filament
- Gold-colored crimp beads
- Hair grip
- Round- and flat-nose pliers
- Wire cutters

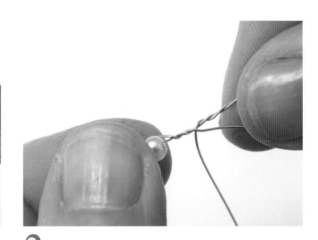

1 Cut four 16-in. (40-cm) lengths of 26-gauge (0.4 mm) gold-plated wire. Place your round-nose pliers in the center of each piece and bend it in half. Where the wires cross, twist them around one another to form a loop. Continue twisting until you have created a twist that is about 1 in. (2.5 cm) long.

2 Separate the wires below the twist and thread one with a pearl bead. Bring the wire around the top of the bead and back toward the bead hole, holding it in place. Carefully twist the wire three or four times around the second wire to make a short stem.

OPPOSITE *This stylish hair grip provides instant glamour for any special occasion.*

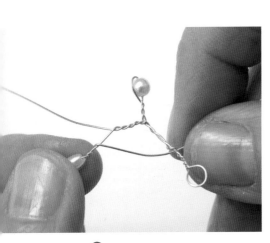

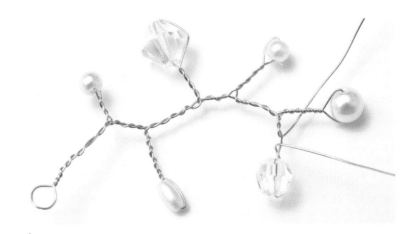

3 Thread another bead onto the other wire and repeat step 2, creating another beaded stem as before.

4 Continue threading the beads and twisting the wires together until you have created a complete beaded "branch" with six or seven stems and a mixture of beads. Repeat steps 1–4 to bead all four pieces of wire that you cut in step 1.

5 Using your flat-nose pliers, squeeze the end loop of each "branch" and twist the wires around in order to obtain fully twisted stems on all four beaded branches.

ABOVE *The beaded tendrils float from the central pearl and add movement and sparkle when worn.*

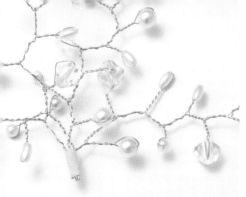

6 Bunch the branches together and tape the stalks together with masking tape. Spend a little time rearranging and shaping the wires into an attractive shape. Where the branches overlap, twist the beads over one another to connect them together, providing the piece with more stability.

7 Using your round-nose pliers, make a ¼-in. (5-mm) coil of 20-gauge (0.8 mm) gold wire, leaving about 1 in. (2.5 cm) of wire extending at one end.

8 Thread the 1 cm pearl feature bead onto this wire. Form a small spiral head pin at the end of the wire (see page 182).

9 Place the taped stems in the coil of wire. Using your flat-nose pliers, squeeze the last ring of the coil tightly against the stems to secure.

10 Cut a 3-in. (7.5-cm) length of 26-gauge (0.4 mm) gold-plated wire and wrap it around the top end of the hair grip and the top of the coil to attach the hair grip to the beaded branches.

11 Cut four 6–8-in. (15–20-cm) lengths of nylon filament. Wrap the center of each filament around the pearl feature bead and the hair grip, and secure by feeding both ends through a gold-colored crimp bead. Push the crimp bead up as far as it will go.

12 Thread the lengths of filament with small pearl, gold bugle, and crystal beads and crimp them in place to create beaded tendrils.

Beaded Bangle

This collection of bangles is colorful and fun, and will instantly brighten up any outfit. You could use a variety of differently colored and shaped beads together, or build up a repeat pattern, as shown here. Wear them on their own or sport several together, in a mixture of colors and styles. And for something a touch more exotic, try suspending some pendant charms intermittently between the beads using jump rings.

YOU WILL NEED

- ❧ 20-gauge (0.8 mm) wire
- ❧ Good selection of beads
- ❧ Round-nose pliers
- ❧ Flat-nose pliers
- ❧ Wire cutters

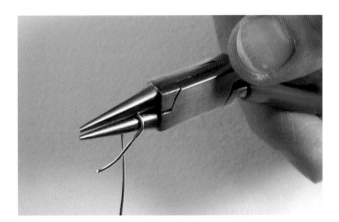

1 To find out how much wire you will require to make the bangle, measure your wrist (a piece of string or cord will do for this) and add approximately 4 in. (10 cm) to this length. Place your round-nose pliers about 1 in. (2.5 cm) from the end of the wire and form a loop by wrapping it around one of the circular shafts.

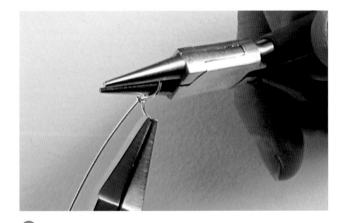

2 Using your flat-nose pliers, wrap the very end of the wire around itself and cut off any excess.

OPPOSITE *The beads are arranged in a repeating pattern, with silver and pale-colored beads interspersed between the more dominant colors to lighten the effect and add a little sparkle.*

3 Thread your chosen beads onto the wire in the desired sequence until you are left with a length of wire measuring approximately 1½–2 in. (4–5 cm). This will be sufficient for your clasp. (Here the colored beads have been separated by tiny silver beads, creating a small space between the brighter colors.)

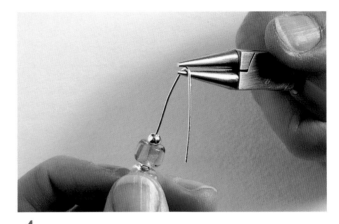

4 To create the clasp, using round-nose pliers, fold the remaining wire so that it is doubled, leaving just enough single-thickness wire to wrap around the bracelet, close to the last bead.

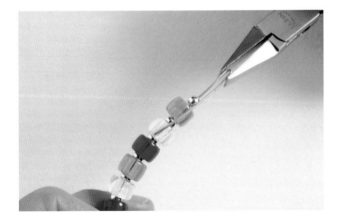

5 Gently squeeze the ends of the two wires together using your flat-nose pliers.

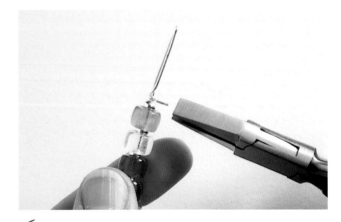

6 Using flat-nose pliers, carefully wind the wire around itself to secure.

7 Fold the wire around your round-nose pliers, about three-quarters of the way up, to form a hook. Bend the very end of this hook into a small lip with the end of your round-nose pliers.

8 Shape the bracelet into a circle by pressing it around a cylindrical object that is smaller in diameter than the bracelet—this gives the bracelet a springiness, enabling it to keep its shape.

VARIATION:
Metallic Bangle

Instead of threading on only beads, you can also use uncut coils of wire jump rings as spacers between the beads to give a different look to your bracelet. This method is particularly good for making extra-special beads stand out. See the instructions on page 182 for making jump rings.

Tassel Clip

This fun key ring or handbag charm also looks fabulous suspended from the end of a belt. Chained tassels are simple to make and can be made into dangly earrings, necklace centerpieces, and bracelet charms. You can also adapt them for home furnishings and sew them onto the corners of pillow covers or the ends of curtain tiebacks.

YOU WILL NEED

- 25-in. (60-cm) length of ready-made chain
- 20-gauge (0.8 mm) and 26-gauge (0.4 mm) silver wire
- 1 x 8 mm turquoise barrel tube bead
- 1 x 4 mm round silver bead
- 1 x 1 cm bicone silver bead
- 5 x size 9/0 turquoise seed beads
- 5 x size 9/0 black seed beads
- Ready-made clip or key-ring finding
- Round- and flat-nose pliers
- Wire cutters

1 Cut ten 2½-in (6-cm) lengths of ready-made chain.

2 Thread the top link of each length of chain onto a 3-in. (7.5-cm) length of 26-gauge (0.4 mm) silver wire.

3 Bring the two ends of the wire together and twist them together to form a short stem about ¼ in. (5 mm) long, above the rows of chain.

OPPOSITE *The chained tassel of this clip adds an air of elegance to any purse or bag. Alternatively, clip it onto the front of a belt loop for a sparkling way of personalizing a pair of mass-produced jeans.*

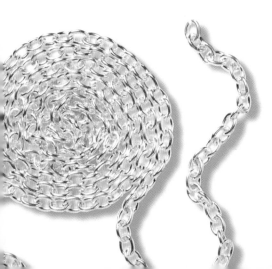

4 Thread the 8 mm turquoise bead and then the 4 mm silver bead onto the twisted stem. Using round- and flat-nose pliers, make a loop with the doubled wire at the top of the bead hole, wrapping the excess wire around the stem to secure.

5 Thread the 1 cm silver bead onto 20-gauge (0.8 mm) silver wire. Using your round-nose pliers, make a link at each end (see page 180).

6 Connect the tassel to one link of the 1 cm silver bead.

7 Thread five black and five turquoise size 9/0 seed beads individually onto 20-gauge (0.8 mm) silver wire. Form a link at one end and a head pin at the other (see pages 180 and 181).

8 Alternating black and turquoise seed beads, attach one seed bead to each section of the chain tassel by opening the link on the seed bead, looping it through the bottom link of one section of chain, and closing the link again with your flat-nose pliers.

9 Connect the top link of the 1 cm bead to the ready-made key ring or clip finding.

VARIATION: Ribbon and Chain Tassel

The tassel can also be created using a mixture of ribbon and chain, which gives a lovely contrast of textures.

Simple Bead Ring

This bright and colorful ring is the kind of design that a young girl would just adore. Although it is very easy to construct, it does look very impressive—purely on account of the beautiful bead in the center. The diameter of the cylindrical dowel that you use to shape the wire in step 1 needs to be slightly smaller than the diameter of your finger, as the wire will spring open and expand slightly.

LEFT These little rings are so easy and quick to make; why not create one to match every outfit in your wardrobe!

YOU WILL NEED

- 20-gauge (0.8 mm) wire
- 26-gauge (0.4 mm) wire for binding
- A cylindrical dowel
- A "feature" bead
- Wire cutters
- Round-nose pliers

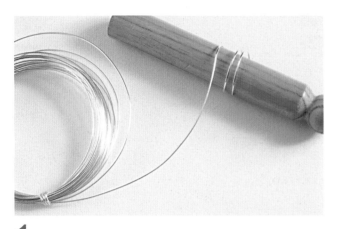

1 Pull out some wire from a 20-gauge (0.8 mm) spool and wrap this twice around the cylindrical dowel. Cut the wire just past the point where it overlaps itself.

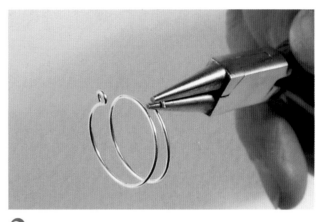

2 Using the tips of your round-nose pliers, curl the ends of the wire back on themselves to form two small, neat loops.

3 Turn these loops 90 degrees, so they sit at right angles to the rest of the ring shank. (If the shank distorts slightly at any stage, simply place it back on the cylindrical dowel and re-shape.)

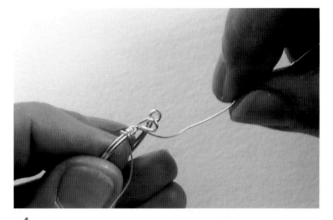

4 Using fine 26-gauge (0.4 mm) wire, begin evenly binding the round shank ¼ in. (6 mm) away from the center of the ring. Do not cut the wire when you have finished binding.

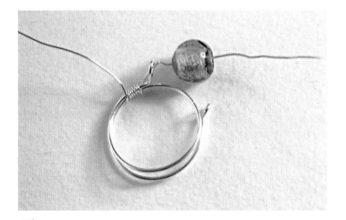

5 Thread the fine wire through one of the loops created in step 2, then thread the wire through the hole in your chosen bead.

6 Continue threading the fine wire through the second loop and finish off by binding around the shank on the other side. If you wish, bind the entire shank.

MASTERING THE ART:
More Advanced Wire and Beadwork

As you progress in jewelry making, you will develop a stronger design sense and get a feeling for how to combine wire and beads together in your work, so that each complements the other. This chapter looks at more advanced wire-working techniques, such as hammering the wire to spread it into flatter shapes (Far Eastern Promise, page 82; Swirling Chain, page 90; Chain of Hearts, page 98).

It also demonstrates using pliers to shape wire into both regular patterns (Wiggly Chain, page 86) and free-flowing, irregular shapes (Golden Tiara, page 102). Finally, there are projects that incorporate classically elegant pendant beads into chain necklaces (Wiggly Chain and Edwardian Necklace, page 106).

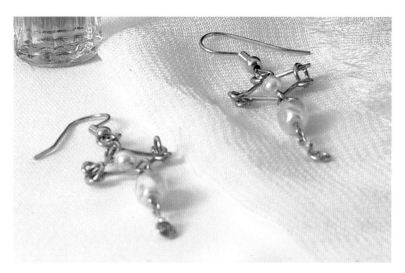

Elegant Eveningwear

Every woman likes to dress up when she goes out for the evening and this chapter contains a range of timeless, understated designs that provide those all-important finishing touches. Suitable for all kinds of occasions, from romantic dinners for two to formal proms and balls, these are sophisticated pieces of jewelry that are guaranteed to make the wearer look and feel like a million dollars.

Far Eastern Promise

With its simple curves, reminiscent of Chinese and Japanese calligraphy, this necklace has a distinct flavor of the Orient. The hammering technique does take practice—but, as they say, practice makes perfect! If you find you've made a real mess of it, shape the ends of the hammered wires into little curls; the result will not look so Oriental, but it still will be very striking!

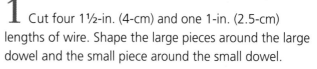

YOU WILL NEED

- ✃ 30 in. (75 cm) 18-gauge (1 mm) silver wire
- ✃ Round- and flat-nose pliers
- ✃ Wire cutters
- ✃ Hammer and flat steel block
- ✃ Dowels 1¼ in. (3 cm) and ¾ in. (2 cm) in diameter

OPPOSITE *Although it takes its inspiration from the ancient art of Oriental calligraphy, this necklace has a distinctly contemporary feel.*

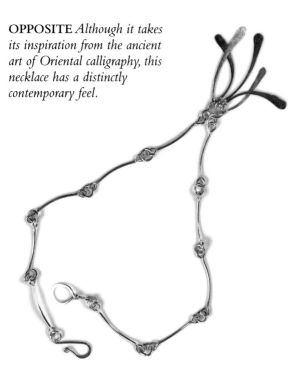

1 Cut four 1½-in. (4-cm) and one 1-in. (2.5-cm) lengths of wire. Shape the large pieces around the large dowel and the small piece around the small dowel.

2 Gently hammer one end of each curved wire on a steel block until it spreads to a bulbous, paddle-shaped tip. Hammer both sides.

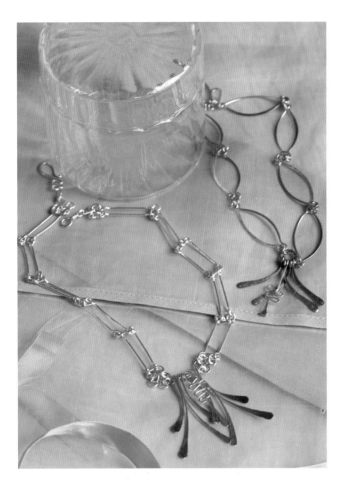

VARIATION:
Hammered Wire Combinations

Experiment with curving and hammering wire to create different shape combinations. You can make more elaborate chains by linking two pieces together as one unit (and in varied metals).

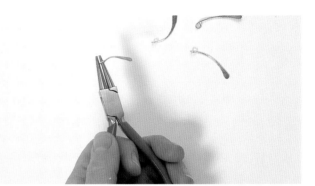

3 Using round-nose pliers, curl the unhammered ends into links, making sure that two sets of links on the longer curves curl one way and two the other. The link on the short piece can curve whichever way you choose.

4 Suspend the curved pieces from a large jump ring, as shown, with the first piece curving outward, the second inward, and the short piece whichever way you choose. The last two pieces should mirror the first.

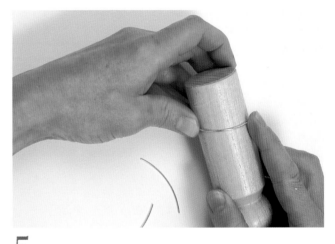

5 Work out how long you want the chain to be. Cut enough 2-in. (5-cm) lengths of 18-gauge (1 mm) wire to make up this length (you will need an odd number of chain units). Curve the pieces around the large dowel.

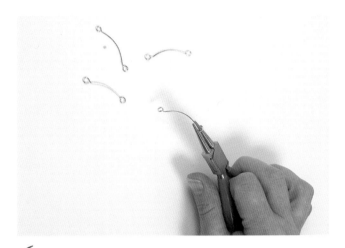

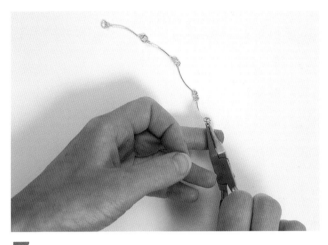

6 Using your round-nose pliers, form a link at each end of each curved piece (see page 180).

7 Join the curved units together with jump rings.

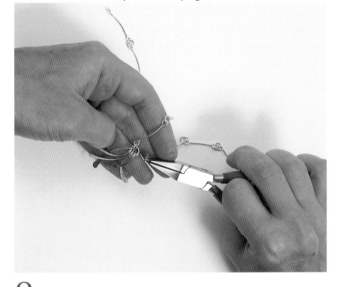

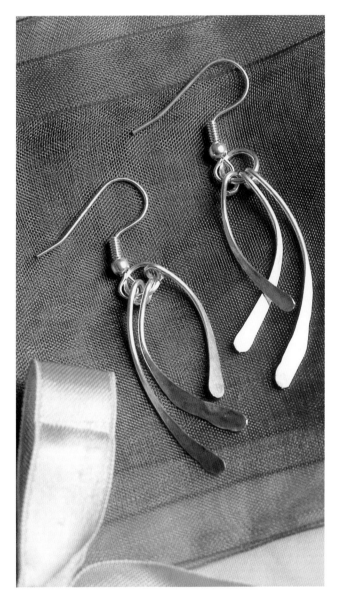

8 Attach the centerpiece to the central jump ring of the chain. Make a clasp (see pages 184–9) and attach it to the ends of the chain.

VARIATION:
Earrings

To make matching earrings, follow steps 1 through 3 and make two 1-in. (2.5-cm) units. Suspend half the curved units on one jump ring and ear wire and half on another.

Wiggly Chain

The semi-translucent beads and open twists of wire make this an incredibly light and delicate-looking necklace. It's virtually impossible to make all the "wiggles" in the wire exactly the same, but it really doesn't matter if there are a few irregularities; it all adds to the individuality and charm of the piece. As you can see from the blue-beaded variation on page 88, it can also be made as a long, continuous necklace without a clasp. Alternatively, try making it without any beads at all, with a smaller version for a matching bracelet.

YOU WILL NEED

- 20-gauge (0.8 mm) silver wire
- Approx. 11 x 7–9 mm oval, beige glass beads
- Round-, chain-, and flat-nose pliers
- Wire cutters
- Hammer and steel stake

OPPOSITE *The pale beads and fine wire units form a striking, yet understated design that suits all ages.*

3 Pull the wire diagonally across the bead back to the first hole, and wrap it around the base of the link to secure. Cut the wire off the spool and neaten up any spiky ends with your chain-nose pliers (see page 187). Repeat steps 1–3 to thread all the beads. The last bead should have a hammered loop, as this will form the "eye" of the clasp in step 12.

1 Working from the spool, thread the first bead with 20-gauge (0.8 mm) wire and form a link at one end (see page 180). Place the center of your round-nose pliers at the other end of the bead and bend the wire at a right angle.

2 Pull the wire over the pliers and wrap it around the stem a couple of times to form a loop.

4 Working from a spool of 20-gauge (0.8 mm) silver wire, make a link at the end of the wire (see page 180) using your round-nose pliers.

(see page 180)

VARIATION
Mix and match different tones and shapes of beads.

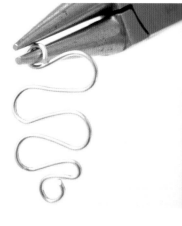

5 Place the tips of your round-nose pliers just under this link and bend the wire around one shaft of the pliers.

6 Move your pliers about ½ in. (1 cm) up the wire and bend the wire around the shaft again, to create a wiggly shape in the wire.

7 Repeat until you have created four more bends. Cut the wire from the spool and, using your round-nose pliers, form a link at the end (see page 180).

(see page 180)

8 Push all the "wiggles" together so that they touch one another, then gently hammer the unit on a steel stake to work harden it (see page 185). Repeat steps 4–8 to make nine more units.

(see page 185)

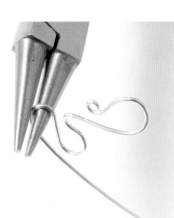

11 Attach the fish-hook clasp to the other end of the necklace.

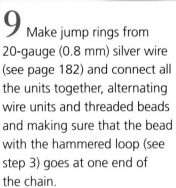

9 Make jump rings from 20-gauge (0.8 mm) silver wire (see page 182) and connect all the units together, alternating wire units and threaded beads and making sure that the bead with the hammered loop (see step 3) goes at one end of the chain.

10 Working from a spool of 20-gauge (0.8 mm) silver wire, make a fish-hook clasp (see page 184) and cut the wire off the spool, leaving 2 in. (5 cm) extending. Shape the stem of the fastener by bending it around the shaft of your round-nose pliers, as in steps 5–7. Gently hammer the fish-hook fastener on a steel stake to work harden it (see page 187).

12 The wrapped loop of the last bead forms the "eye" of the fastener, although the fish-hook fastener can be connected anywhere within the necklace to make it shorter if you prefer.

RIGHT *The semi-translucent glass beads and delicate silver chain units give this necklace a thoroughly feminine feel.*

Swirling Chain

This chain—an apparently seamless circle of swirling spirals—has a classic, timeless quality. It is fastened by simply opening one of the loops in the last chain unit slightly and hooking it over the first chain, as I felt that a conventional hook-and-eye fastener would break the circle and disrupt the unity of the piece. The spiral units are hammered to flatten and spread the wire slightly, which gives the chain a lovely delicate appearance; had the spirals been left unhammered, the piece would have had a much more mechanical, mass-produced feel.

YOU WILL NEED
- 20-gauge (0.8 mm) silver wire
- Round- and flat-nose pliers
- Wire cutters
- Hammer and steel stake

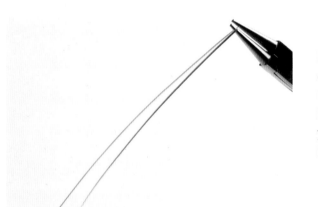

1 Cut 11 9-in. (23-cm) lengths of 20-gauge (0.8 mm) silver wire. Bend each length in half by placing the tips of your round-nose pliers in the center.

OPPOSITE *These swirling silver spirals form a continuous chain necklace that would set off a classic "little black dress" to perfection.*

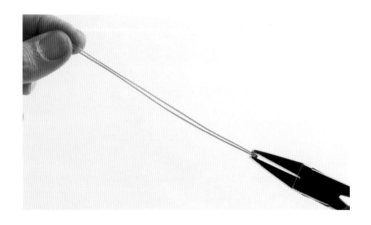

2 Squeeze the doubled-over end of wire with your flat-nose pliers and pull the wires with your fingers so that they run straight and parallel to one another.

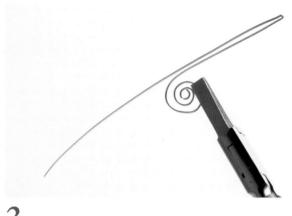

3 Using your round-nose pliers, curl one end of the wire into a circle. Hold the circle firmly in the jaws of your flat-nose pliers, then curl the wire outward into an open spiral, leaving about 1½ in. (4 cm) of wire unspiraled.

4 Form another open spiral on the other side, spiraling it outward as before, so that it sits just below the first.

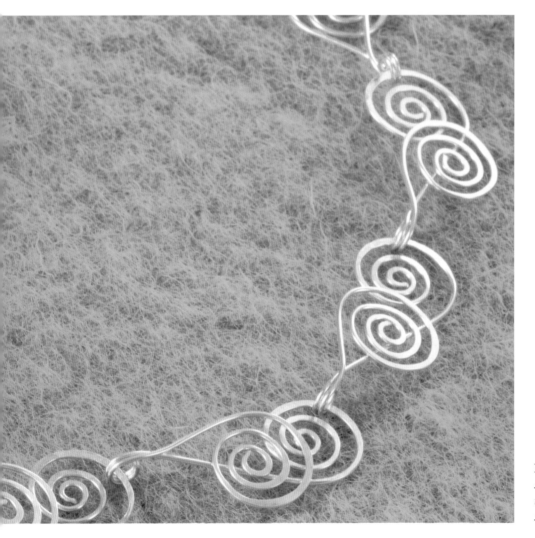

LEFT *This close-up photograph shows more clearly the interlocking system of the swirling wire units.*

5 Hammer both spirals on a steel stake to flatten and work harden them (see page 185)—but take care not to hammer the doubled-over end of the wire.

6 Place the fattest part of your round-nose pliers at the end of the doubled wire and curl the wire forward, to form a complete circle at 90° to the spirals. Make this link on ten of the 11 units. On the final unit, leave the link slightly ajar as this will form the clasp.

7 Push both spirals in toward each other, so that they sit above one another. The wire is very springy, so you will need to push the top spiral just past the bottom one as it will spring back to sit in the correct position.

8 Connect all 11 units together by linking one end into the other to form a chain.

9 Hook the last unit with the slightly open link onto the last spiral to act as an invisible clasp.

Pearly Necklace

This design of beautiful pearl beads on gold wire harks back to the turn of the nineteenth century and would make a stunning accessory for a low–cut evening dress. This color combination would also look fantastic against an ivory-colored wedding dress. For an alternative color scheme, use clear crystals or colored Swarovski beads.

YOU WILL NEED

- ❧ 20-gauge (0.8 mm) gold wire
- ❧ 6 x 5 mm pearls
- ❧ 1 x 1 cm pearl
- ❧ 24 x size 9/0 white pearl seed beads
- ❧ 8 x size 9/0 gold seed beads
- ❧ Round- and flat-nose pliers
- ❧ Wire cutters
- ❧ Hammer and steel stake

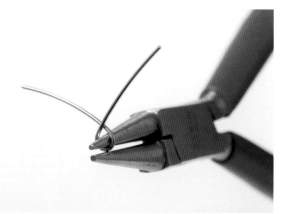

1 To make the central hanger of the necklace, cut a 2-in. (5-cm) length of 20-gauge (0.8 mm) gold wire. Find the center of the wire with your round-nose pliers and wrap the wires around one of the circular shafts, crossing the wires over in opposite directions to form a central loop.

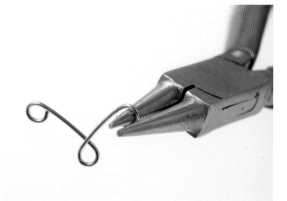

2 Using your round-nose pliers, create a small link at each end of the wire, curling outward in opposite directions (see page 180).

OPPOSITE *Gold and pearls—a classic combination. To make matching earrings, follow step 8 of the necklace, add seed beads to the wire stems, and connect the threaded beads onto ready-made ear wires.*

3 Hammer the unit on a steel stake to work harden it, taking care not to touch the crossed-over wires as this will weaken them.

4 To make the chain, cut 24 1½-in. (4-cm) lengths of 20-gauge (0.8 mm) gold wire. Thread a pearl seed bead onto each length and form a beaded S-link.

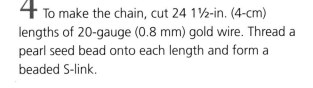

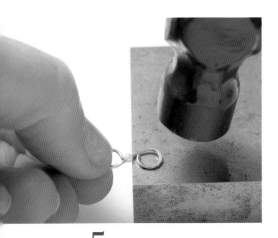

5 Stroke hammer the ends of each unit on a steel stake (see page 187), making sure you do not hammer the beads.

6 Make 26 jump rings (see page 182). Starting and ending with a jump ring, connect the beaded S-links together in two sections of 12 units each.

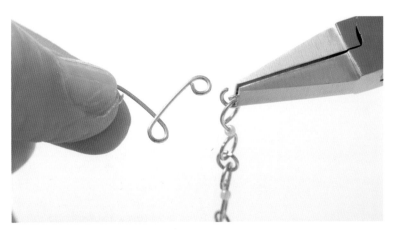

7 Attach one end of each section of chain to the central hanger that you made earlier in steps 1–3.

8 Cut six 1-in. (2.5-cm) lengths of 20-gauge (0.8 mm) gold wire and form a head pin at one end of each length. Thread each wire with a gold seed bead, followed by a 5 mm pearl bead. Using your round-nose pliers, make a link at the opposite end of the wire (see page 180), leaving a little stem just under ¼ in. (5 mm) long.

9 Cut a 1½-in. (4-cm) length of 20-gauge (0.8 mm) gold wire and form a head pin at one end (see page 181). Thread on one gold seed bead, the 1 cm pearl and another gold seed bead. Form a link at the other end of the wire.

10 Connect the large pearl to the central loop of the hanger, with three of the smaller, 5 mm pearls on each side, linked into the jump rings in between the S-links.

VARIATION:
Single Focal Bead
This variation has just one focal bead, with the "hanger" frame threaded with pearl seed beads.

11 To complete the necklace, make an S-clasp (see page 186), and attach it to one end of the necklace. You do not need to make a separate eye for the fastener, as the S-link clasp is simply hooked into any beaded S-link, so the length of the necklace can be adjusted to suit the wearer.

Chain of Hearts

The pinkish tone of the copper wire used to make this chain is intended to evoke Cupid, the chubby, pink cherub of love who strikes us with his loaded arrows just when we're least expecting it! This continuous chain-link design would work equally well as a bracelet. Alternatively, to make matching earrings, simply add delicate little beads to the heart-shaped units and suspend them from ready-made ear wires.

OPPOSITE *This delicate-looking chain is dressy without being overly formal or fussy.*

YOU WILL NEED

- ✂ 20-gauge (0.8 mm) copper wire
- ✂ Round- and flat-nose pliers
- ✂ Wire cutters
- ✂ Hammer and steel stake

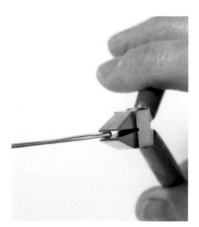

1 For a 16-in. (40-cm) chain, cut 18–20 pieces of 20-gauge (0.8 mm) copper wire 4–4½ in. (10–12 cm) long. Fold each wire in half. Squeeze the end of the doubled wires together with your flat-nose pliers and straighten out the wires with your fingers so that they run parallel to one another.

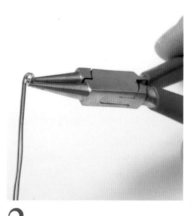

2 Using the tips of your round-nose pliers, curl a small loop at the doubled-over end of the wire, curling the wire toward you so that the loop is at right angles to the straight wires.

3 Holding the doubled loop firmly in your flat-nose pliers, gently pull the two wires apart.

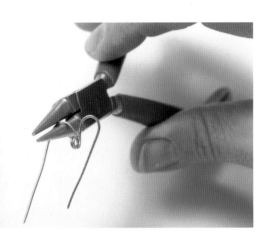

4 Place the widest part of your round-nose pliers on each side of the doubled loop and bring the wires back down until they meet and cross over, forming a heart-shaped frame.

5 Gently stroke hammer the round shoulders of the frame, taking care not to hammer and squash the doubled loop (see page 187).

6 Wrap one of the extending wires at the base of the heart two or three times around the other. Snip off any excess wrapped wire and squeeze the end flat against the stem with your flat-nose pliers to neaten, leaving the other wire extending.

7 Using your round-nose pliers, form a link (see page 180) at the end of the extending wire. Repeat steps 1–7 to make 18–20 heart-shaped units.

8 Open the link at the base of one heart and loop it through the doubled-over loop of wire at the top of the next heart. Close the link again, using your flat-nose pliers.

9 Repeat until you have connected all the heart units together in a continuous chain.

10 To complete the necklace, make a fishhook clasp and a wrapped eye (see pages 184 and 186) from 20-gauge (0.8 mm) copper wire and attach to the ends of the necklace.

VARIATION:
Matching Earrings

To make matching earrings, follow steps 1–6 of the chain. Then, instead of forming a link at the base of the heart, thread one 3–4-mm bead onto the extending wire and form a spiral head pin (see page 182) at the very end of the wire.

Thread another bead onto a 1-in. (2.5-cm) length 20-gauge (0.8 mm) copper wire, and form a link at one end and a head pin at the other (see page 181).

Connect three jump rings together to form a small chain (see page 183), loop the top jump ring through the doubled loop at the top of the heart-shaped unit, and suspend the threaded bead from the bottom jump ring.

Golden Tiara

For a really formal evening occasion—a grand ball, perhaps, or a night at the opera—a stylish tiara is guaranteed to impress. This version features different sizes of gold and silver beads atop a silver base, and would work equally well as a bridal headpiece—a surefire way of making the bride feel like a princess for her special day. Other beautiful bead combinations would be freshwater pearls and crystal beads, or ivory and salmon pearls. Although the design looks complex, it is actually relatively simple to make.

I hope it will spark off ideas for a headpiece using beads and color combinations of your choice.

YOU WILL NEED

- ❦ 20-gauge (0.8 mm) silver wire
- ❦ 26-gauge (0.4 mm) gold wire
- ❦ Tiara band
- ❦ Approx. 80 x size 9/0 silver seed beads
- ❦ Approx. 16 x 4 mm gold-plated beads
- ❦ Approx. 16 x 6 mm gold-plated beads
- ❦ Round- and flat-nose pliers
- ❦ Wire cutters

OPPOSITE *This tiara can be made using any color of bead. For a bolder crown, form higher peaks and thread with larger beads.*

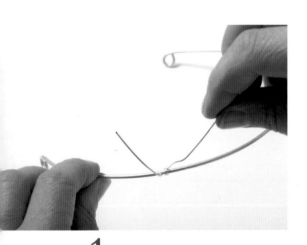

1 Cut approximately 24–30 in. (60–75 cm) of 20-gauge (0.8 mm) silver wire. Leaving about 1 in. (2.5 cm) of wire extending, and starting about 4 in. (10 cm) in from the end of the tiara frame, wrap the wire two or three times tightly around the frame to secure.

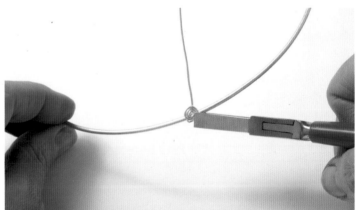

2 Form a small, closed spiral at the end of the extending wire (see page 182). Flatten the spiral against the frame to hide the wrapped wire underneath, and press it down with your flat-nose pliers.

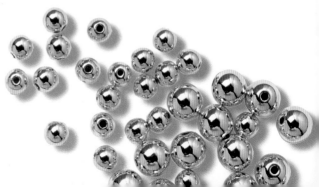

VARIATIONS

Both of variations shown above demonstrate how easily you can adapt this project. The tiara on the left has red and silver beads, while the pearl and crystal tiara has been wired with extra stalks of wire threaded with more pearl beads, secured with Superglue at the tips.

3 Thread on a 6 mm gold bead, then bend the wire around the tips of your round-nose pliers to form a peak.

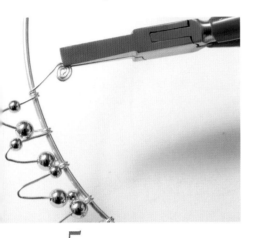

4 Thread on a 4 mm gold bead and secure by wrapping the wire once around the frame. Continue, adding 6 mm and 4 mm gold beads to each peak as you work. The peaks do not have to be symmetrical.

5 When you are about 1½ in. (4 cm) from the end of the frame, wrap the wire a couple of times around the frame to secure. Form a small, closed spiral, as in step 2, and flatten it against the wrapped wires to conceal them.

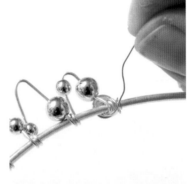

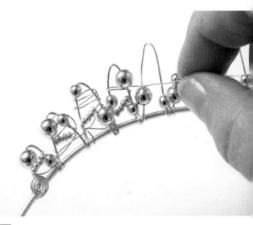

6 Cut about 24 in. (60 cm) of 26-gauge (0.4 mm) gold wire and wrap it underneath one of the side spirals to secure.

7 Continue wrapping this thinner gold wire around the framework, threading it randomly with silver seed beads. If you run out of wire, just cut some more and continue wrapping.

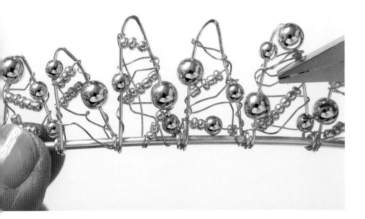

8 Continue filling the wiggly peaks with wrapped wire and beads until you are satisfied with the effect. Spend a little time readjusting your tiara framework using your fingers and flat-nose pliers, and make sure that the wire peaks are centered on the tiara frame.

Edwardian Necklace

The style of this necklace harks back to the Edwardian period of the early twentieth century and features a dramatic pendant above a "tassel" of gold-and-pearl strands. It uses a ready-made chain and would be the ideal embellishment for any style of formal dress with a low neckline. For a necklace with a higher neckline, omit the tassel (steps 9 and 10). If you wish, for a special finishing touch, make your own chain. You could also substitute crystal beads for the pearls and silver wire for the gold.

YOU WILL NEED

- ❧ Ready-made chain—enough to fit around your neck and large enough to thread 24-gauge (0.6 mm) wire through the links
- ❧ 20-gauge (0.8 mm) gold-plated wire
- ❧ 5 tiny pearl beads
- ❧ 2 larger pearl beads
- ❧ Wire cutters
- ❧ Round-nose pliers

OPPOSITE *This combination of gold and pearls has a classic, timeless feel and looks incredibly luxurious.*

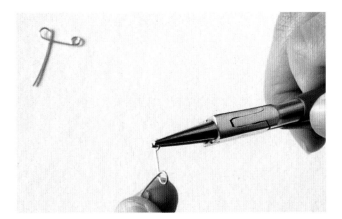

1 The central beaded pendant is constructed first. To make this, cut two 2-in. (5-cm) lengths of 20-gauge (0.8 mm) gold-plated wire.

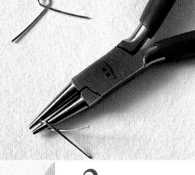

2 Using round-nose pliers, find the center of each wire and cross one side over the other to create a central loop.

3 Curl the extended ends outward into small loops using the ends of the round-nose pliers. These will make up the two halves of the pendant.

4 Create jump rings to link the pendant together by wrapping 20-gauge (0.8 mm) wire around the round-nose pliers to form a coil (see page 182). Cut each ring of the coil to create the links (see inset).

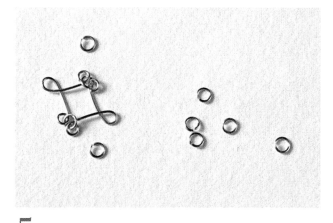

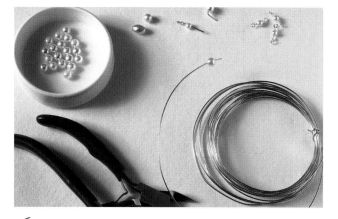

5 Connect the two halves of the pendant together on each side using the jump rings you have just made.

6 Thread the bead for the center of the pendant onto 20-gauge (0.8 mm) wire, leaving ½ in. (1 cm) of wire on either side. Fold each wire end into a right angle, then back to form a loop. Do this on both sides and attach the loops to the top and bottom of the pendant.

7 To make the hanging beads on either side of the pendant, thread two smaller beads onto 20-gauge (0.8 mm) wire, leaving ½ in. (1 cm) of wire on one side, and a little less on the other to form a head pin (see page 181). Attach these in the same way as in step 6.

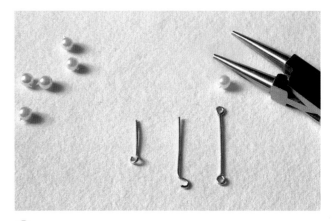

8 For the drop bead, thread a larger pearl onto 20-gauge (0.8 mm) wire, forming links at both ends with your round-nose pliers, as you did in step 6. Connect this to the bottom loop of the pendant.

9 To make the tassel, cut three lengths of 20-gauge (0.8 mm) wire, graduating from about 1½ in. (4 cm) down. Form small loops at the ends of each length using the very end of the round-nose pliers.

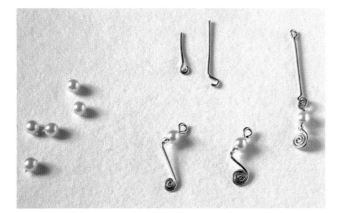

10 Thread three small beads onto 20-gauge (0.8 mm) wire, leaving ½ in. (1 cm) at one end to form a link and at least 1½ in. (4 cm) at the other end to curl into a spiral. Connect all three spiraled pearls onto the tassel sticks to form the center of your necklace.

11 Link this unit to the center of the chain. You may need to create some small jump rings out of 24-gauge (0.6 mm) wire to connect onto the links of the chain (see page 182).

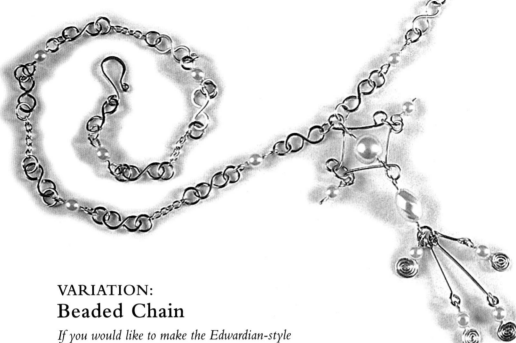

VARIATION:
Beaded Chain

If you would like to make the Edwardian-style necklace more decorative (perhaps if your dress is a classic, simple design), you can create a more elaborate chain by using S-links interspersed at regular intervals with threaded beads (see pages 180 and 186).

VARIATION:
Drop Earrings

To create drop earrings to match the necklace, simply follow steps 1–10 of the necklace and suspend the tops of the hangers from gold ear wires.

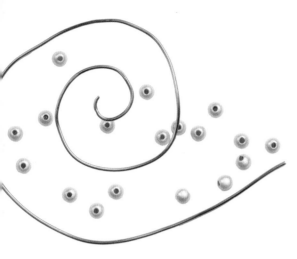

Wavy Chain

This chain unit has been one of my favorites for many years. Here I have given it a Celtic twist by extending the ends of the curved units into spirals.

Scotland and Ireland were the heartlands of Celtic civilization, and the coastal areas of these two countries have some of the most dramatic scenery. This design is intended to evoke the waves hitting the cliffs, with the blue-green wire representing the waves and the silver wire representing the hard granite of the rocks.

YOU WILL NEED

- ✂ 20-gauge (0.8 mm) silver wire
- ✂ 20-gauge (0.8 mm) green wire
- ✂ 24-gauge (0.6 mm) silver wire
- ✂ 40 x 5 mm silver beads
- ✂ Round- and flat-nose pliers
- ✂ Wire cutters
- ✂ Cylindrical dowel 1 in. (2.5 cm) in diameter

1 Cut ten 3-in. (7.5-cm) lengths of 20-gauge (0.8 mm) silver wire and ten lengths of green. Find the center of each piece and bend it around a cylindrical dowel to curve it into a shallow "U"-shape.

2 Using the tips of your round-nose pliers, curl one end of each unit into a small circle. Thread two 5 mm silver beads onto the other end of the wire.

OPPOSITE *This highly decorative chain necklace is made using two contrasting colors of wire, with pearly silver beads adding fullness to the piece. Try making the chain with smaller spirals and without beads; you'll be amazed at how different it can look!*

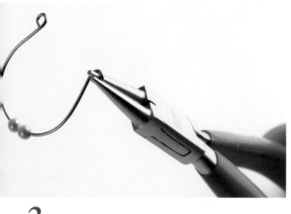

3 Curl another small circle on the other side of the curved wire.

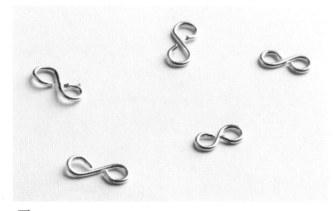

5 Next, cut 21 ½-in. (1-cm) pieces of 24-gauge (0.6 mm) silver wire. Using the tips of your round-nose pliers, form a circle at each end of each piece, curling them in opposite directions to make a figure-of-eight.

4 Form a small, tight spiral (see page 182) at each end of the wire, curling the wires inward, until you are left with about 1 in. (2.5 cm) of unspiraled wire, with the two beads at the center.

6 To join the units together, open one side of a figure-of-eight piece and attach it to one of the green curved units, between the two beads. Attach the other side of the figure-of-eight piece to a silver unit in the same way, making sure that both curves face inward.

7 Repeat step 6 until you have linked all the units together and formed a chain, alternating the colors as shown.

OPPOSITE *This silver wire and gold bead version of the Wavy Chain would look stunning for a formal occasion. Alternatively, a combination of gold wire and pearls would be the perfect complement for a bridal dress.*

8 To complete, make a fish-hook clasp and eye (see pages 184 and 186).

Spiral Ring

Tendrils of curling spirals radiate out from this ring in an eye-catching, free-flowing design. With a dramatic blood-red bead at its center, it is very decorative—but if you would prefer a plainer look, you could make it with fewer spirals and omit the focal bead. Alternatively, add a smaller, cube-shaped bead to every tendril and twist the spiral ends in different directions for a complete design transformation. The ring will fit most finger sizes, as it has a front opening.

YOU WILL NEED

- 20-gauge (0.8 mm) and 24-gauge (0.6 mm) silver wire
- 1 x red oval bead, 10 mm x 6 mm
- Round- and flat-nose pliers
- Wire cutters
- Ring mandrel or cylindrical dowel
- Hammer

1 Cut three 5-in. (12.5-cm) lengths of 20-gauge (0.8 mm) silver wire and straighten them so that they are parallel to each other. Cut two 2½-in. (6-cm) lengths of 24-gauge (0.6 mm) silver wire. Hold the three thicker wires together, making sure they sit in a line, one above the other. Take one piece of the thinner wire and use it to bind the thicker wires together about 1½ in. (4 cm) from one end.

2 Repeat on the other side. Squeeze the ends of the wrapped wires with your flat-nose pliers to tighten them against the thicker wires.

OPPOSITE *This very distinctive, dressy ring design looks fantastic with any color of focal bead. As the alternative designs in the background show, it can be made with more beads or with no beads at all!*

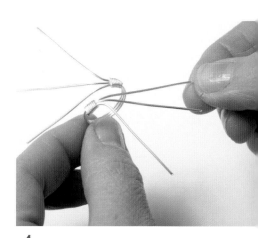

3 Mold the wrapped wires around a ring mandrel to shape them into a circular ring shank, overlapping the ends, one above the other. If you do not have a ring mandrel, use a piece of wooden dowel or narrow curtain pole.

4 Using your fingers, separate the three wires on each side and spread them out in a fan shape.

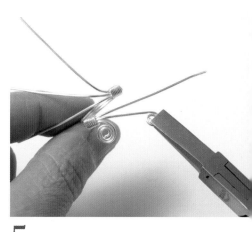

5 On one side, form a small loop at the end of each wire with your round-nose pliers, and then use your flat-nose pliers to create a closed spiral (see page 182).

VARIATION:
Beadless Ring

Omit the beads and push the outer spirals in toward the center, in order to cover the wrapped wires on the ring shank.

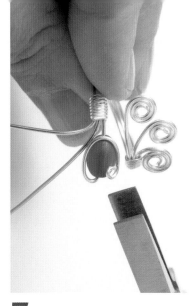

6 On the other side of the fan, thread the red oval bead onto the first extending wire and push it right up against the wrapped wire frame. Bend the extending wire around the perimeter of the bead.

7 Using your round-nose pliers, make a small loop at the very end of the wire and push it flat against the bead.

8 Repeat step 5 to create a closed spiral at the end of the remaining two wires.

9 Place the ring back on the mandrel to reshape it. Press the spirals flat against the mandrel. Stroke hammer the spirals and the back of the ring to work harden them (see page 185).

VARIATION:
Lots of Beads

Thread all the projecting wires with small cube-shaped beads.

ENHANCING YOUR SKILLS:
Beaded Motifs and Variations

From free-flowing, abstract designs, you are now ready to move on to creating beaded motifs. This chapter includes hearts (Sweetheart Necklace, page 138), insects (the dragonfly on the Bridesmaid's Wand, page 126, and the Butterfly Necklace, page 135), and flowers (Flower Cuff, page 123), but you can use the same techniques with anything that has a strong, instantly recognizable outline shape. Some of the projects also feature cord or ribbon (Summer Seashell Necklace, page 131, and the Sweetheart Necklace); these make informal-looking foundations for necklaces and bracelets and are particularly suitable for pieces of jewelry for young girls.

Gorgeous and Girly

This chapter features pieces of jewelry designed specifically for little girls and the decidedly young at heart! Many of the designs are made using colored wire and beads in pretty pastel shades and are inspired by elements of the natural world. All are simple to create and make lovely gifts for little princesses everywhere.

Flower Cuff

I used two tones of pink for the decorative flowers in this bangle, but you could use a single color (or more!) if you prefer. This design will give you a base pattern from which to make a wide variety of bangles, using beads, colored wire motifs, or even colored buttons. Not only is it a fun piece of jewelry, but it also works well as a napkin ring or as a decorative ring around a glass jar, bottle, or pot.

OPPOSITE *Pink and perky, this colorful little flower bangle is the perfect piece of spring- or summertime jewelry. Why not make several, in different colors, to match different outfits?*

YOU WILL NEED

- ⚜ 12-gauge (2 mm), 20-gauge (0.8 mm), and 26-gauge (0.4 mm) silver wire
- ⚜ 20-gauge (0.8 mm) dark pink and light pink wire
- ⚜ Round- and flat-nose pliers
- ⚜ Heavy-duty and standard wire cutters
- ⚜ Hammer and steel stake
- ⚜ Mandrel or other cylindrical object about 2½ in. (6 cm) in diameter

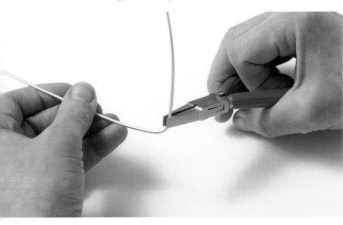

1 Cut a 18-in. (45-cm) length of 12-gauge (2 mm) silver wire. Find the center and, holding it firmly in your flat-nose pliers, bend the wire at an angle of 90°.

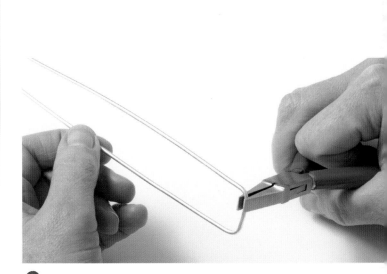

2 Move your pliers about ½ in. (1 cm) along the wire and bend the wire up at 90° again. Using your fingers, straighten both projecting wires so that they run parallel to each other.

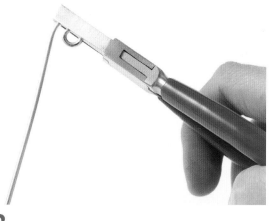

3 At the end of each projecting wire, form an open spiral about ¾ in. (2 cm) in diameter (see page 182). The spirals should curl outward, in opposite directions.

4 Mold the wire around a mandrel or other cylindrical object about 21½ in. (6 cm) in diameter (or large enough to fit your wrist), to shape it into a circular bangle.

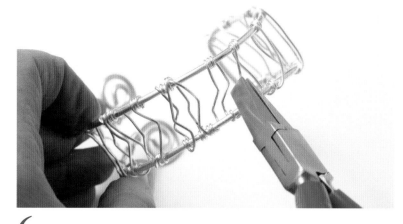

6 Using the tips of your flat-nose pliers, twist and bend the zig-zagged wire into interesting shapes.

5 Cut a 20-in. (50-cm) length of 20-gauge (0.8 mm) silver wire and wrap it around the ends of the spirals to hold the bangle in shape. Continue wrapping the wire along the top and bottom of the frame in an uneven zig-zag pattern, wrapping it two or three times around the frame each time, until you have filled the space. Cut more wire if necessary.

7 Now make the colored wire flowers out of 20-gauge (0.8 mm) pink wire. Working from the spool, form a loop around the shaft of your round-nose pliers about 1 in. (2.5 cm) from the end of the wire.

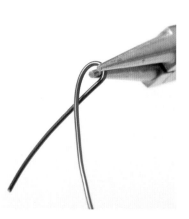

8 Cross the wire over the first loop and make a second loop, opposite the first.

9 Repeat the process, looping the wire around the pliers so that the loops sit opposite each other each time, until you have five or six "petals." Cut the wire off the spool, leaving about 1½ in. (4 cm) extending. Turn the flower shape over and wrap the short end of wire (left from making the first loop in step 7) around the center of the flower.

10 Press the wrapped wire flat with your flat-nose pliers to secure. Cut off any excess and neaten the ends (see page 187). Using your fingers, carefully adjust the petals so that they are evenly spaced.

11 Using the tips of your round-nose pliers, curl a hook at the end of the extending wire. Using your flat-nose pliers, squeeze the hook onto the extending wire like a head pin, and then continue coiling the wire around itself to create a tight spiral. Press the spiral onto the center of the flower. Repeat steps 7–11 to make nine flowers in total—four from dark pink and five from light pink wire.

12 Alternating light and dark pink flowers, bind the flowers to the bangle with 26-gauge (0.4 mm) silver wire. Snip off any excess binding wire and neaten the ends.

VARIATIONS:
Color Changes

Make the flowers and frame in different colors or wire beads to the flower centers.

Bridesmaid's Wand

Every little girl dreams of being a bridesmaid! The beauty of a wand, as opposed to a posy of fresh flowers, is that you can make it well in advance and know that you won't have to worry about flowers wilting—and the bridesmaid can keep and treasure it as a reminder of a very special day. Use wire and beads in a color that matches the bridesmaids' dresses. Other beaded motifs—perhaps butterflies, hearts, or flowers—can be suspended from the top hooks in place of the dragonfly shown here.

YOU WILL NEED

- 12-gauge (2 mm) pink wire
- 20-gauge (0.8 mm) wire in two tones of pink
- 24-gauge (0.6 mm) fuchsia pink wire
- 100 x size 9/0 pink seed beads
- 90 x size 9/0 pearl seed beads
- Round- and flat-nose pliers
- Wire cutters
- Hammer and steel stake
- Mandrel or cylindrical dowel ½ in. (1 cm) in diameter

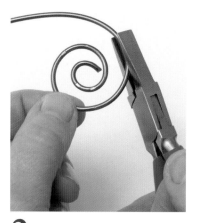

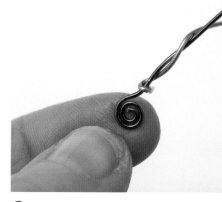

1 Cut a 14–16-in. (35–40-cm) length of 12-gauge (2 mm) pink wire for the wand stem. Using your round-nose pliers, form a loop at one end. Place the mandrel just below the loop and bend the wire about halfway around it in the opposite direction to form a shape like a shepherd's crook.

2 Using your round- and flat-nose pliers, form an open spiral at the other end of the wire (see page 182). Hammer the top loop and the base spiral on a steel stake to work harden the wire (see page 185).

3 To make the dragonfly, cut a 6-in. (15-cm) length of the first tone of 20-gauge (0.8 mm) pink wire. Using your round-nose pliers, form a small closed spiral at one end (see page 16). Cut a 6½-in. (16-cm) length of the second tone of 20-gauge (0.8 mm) pink wire and wrap it around the top of the spiral to secure. Continue wrapping it around the stem wire for just over 1 in. (2.5 cm).

OPPOSITE *These pretty wands are the perfect accessory for very young flower girls as they are light and easy to carry.*

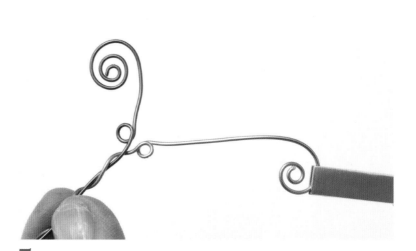

4 Using the tips of your round-nose pliers, curl a small loop, curling outward, in each wire, just below the end of the twist. Straighten and pull the loops up to make the dragonfly's "eyes."

5 Using your round-nose pliers, curl a small circle at the end of each projecting wire. Hold the circle tightly in your flat-nose pliers and form open spirals, curling in opposite directions, for the dragonfly's "antennae."

6 Cut a 20-in. (50-cm) length of 24-gauge (0.6 mm) fuchsia pink wire. Wrap it two or three times around the stem, leaving the same amount of wire extending on each side of the dragonfly's body. Thread 40 pink seed beads onto one end and bend it into a loop to make the first wing. Wrap the wire two or three times around the dragonfly's body, but do not cut off the excess.

7 Thread the remainder of the same wire with 40 pink seed beads and secure as before, to form a second wing on the other side of the dragonfly's body. Do not cut off the excess wire.

8 Repeat steps 9 and 10, threading the other extending wire with pearl seed beads to form a second row of dragonfly wings.

9 Pull one of the projecting wires up into the center and wrap it around the body, just under the eyes, leaving approximately 1 in. (2.5 cm) extending.

10 Using your round-nose pliers, form a link by curling the end of the wire around the circular shaft until it sits between the eyes and the antennae.

11 Thread the remaining projecting wire with seed beads, alternating two pink beads with one pearl, until you are left with just 1 in. (2.5 cm) of wire extending. At the end of the wire form a small spiral (see page 182), leaving a ¼-in. (5-mm) gap between the spiral and the beads. Hold the spiral in your fingers and curl the beaded wire into a spiral, then flatten it against the dragonfly's body with your fingers.

12 Decorate the stem of the wand by wrapping it with 20-gauge (0.8 mm) pale pink wire or ribbon.

13 Using 12-gauge (2 mm) wire, make an S-link. Loop one end of the S-link through the loop that you made in step 10, and attach the other end through the loop that is at the top of the wand.

Summer Seashell Necklace

With its pale, sun-bleached colors, this casual corded necklace has a lovely summery feel—the perfect way to show off a light tan! You can buy pre-drilled shells from bead suppliers. Alternatively, use shells that you've picked up from the beach; place a piece of masking tape over the shell and carefully drill through with a very fine drill bit—and expect some breakages, as shells are incredibly fragile. The necklace is fastened by attaching the fish-hook clasp to any point between the knots in the cord.

YOU WILL NEED

- 60 in. (150 cm) natural-colored coated cotton cord
- 30–40 assorted shells
- Approx. 15 size 8/0 turquoise seed beads
- 24-gauge (0.6 mm) and 20-gauge (0.8 mm) silver wire
- Superglue (optional)
- Round- and flat-nose pliers
- Wire cutters
- Hammer and steel block (optional)

1 To make the eye for the fish-hook clasp, wrap 20-gauge (0.8 mm) wire around the tip of your round-nose pliers ten to twelve times to make a tight, even coil about ¼ in. (6 mm) long. The coil needs to be wide enough to slide onto doubled-up cord. Alternatively, wrap the wire around a knitting needle or a mandrel.

OPPOSITE *These delicate little shell beads simply cry out to be strung on natural-colored cord or leather: a metal chain would look far too heavy.*

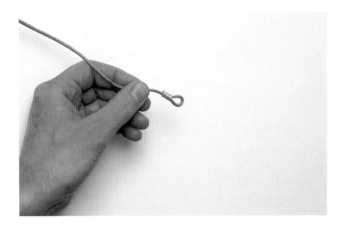

2 Cut cord three times as long as you want the necklace to be. Slide the wire coil onto the cord. Feed the cord back on itself, through the coil, to form a loop.

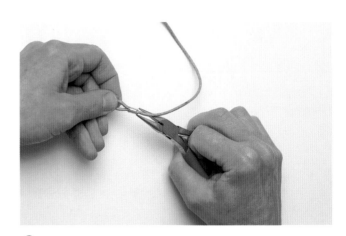

3 Using flat-nose pliers, squeeze the first and last loop of the coil tightly onto the cord to fix it firmly in place. If you wish, add a little Superglue for extra strength.

4 Thread the shells with 24-gauge (0.6 mm) wire, forming a head pin at one end and a link at the other (see pages 180 and 181). Thread several small shells onto one wire and add turquoise seed beads.

5 Make jump rings (see page 182) from 20-gauge (0.8mm) wire and loop them through the top links of the shells. Fasten the jump rings around the cord and close with flat-nose pliers, knotting the cord on each side to hold the shells in position. In places, group two or three shells together for added fullness.

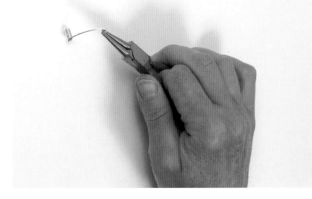

6 Following the instructions in step 1, make a coil of wire that is just wide enough to slip over the cord, leaving about 1 in. (2.5 cm) protruding. With your round-nose pliers, curl a tiny loop at the end of the protruding wire.

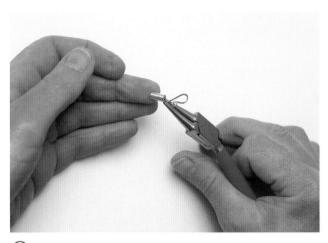

7 Place the widest part of the round-nose pliers under the loop, and form a fish-hook clasp (see page 184).

8 Bend the fish-hook clasp so that it sits vertically above the coil. Work-harden the hook (see page 185).

9 Slide the clasp onto the end of the cord and squeeze the last loop of the coil with flat-nose pliers.

10 Using jump rings, connect and suspend a bunch of linked shells from the end of the loop.

VARIATION:
Colored Glass Beads

Cord comes in many different colors. Thread beads onto colored wires to coordinate with whatever color of cord you are using.

Butterfly Necklace

This beaded butterfly motif is very simple to make. I opted for a bold, graphic color scheme of black and green, but you could take your inspiration from brightly colored butterflies in zingy, tropical shades and make a silver body and antennae for a lighter, more frivolous look. Use the same motif on a brooch—or even wire butterflies onto plant sticks, so that they can flutter amongst the pots in your garden!

YOU WILL NEED

- 24-gauge (0.6 mm) black iron wire
- Approx. 100 size 8/0 green and black seed beads
- 1 x 5 mm green wood bead
- Tan, black, and green ¼ in. (0.5 mm) cord
- Masking tape
- Round- and flat-nose pliers
- Wire cutters
- Hammer and steel block
- Vise
- Superglue (optional)

1 Using your round-nosed pliers, make a ¼-in. (5-mm) coil of 24-gauge (0.6 mm) black wire, in the same way as when making jump rings (see page 182). Holding the top two rings on each side with your fingers, stretch it out to about 1 in. (2.5 cm) in length.

2 Cut a 6–8-in. (15–20-cm) length of black wire. Find the center and bend the wire around one of the shafts of your round-nose pliers. At the point where the wire meets around the shaft of the pliers, pinch the wire with the tips of your flat-nose pliers to form a loop, with both ends of the wire running parallel to each other.

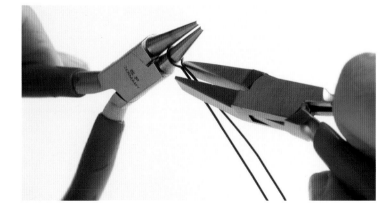

OPPOSITE *Make this black-wire butterfly in your favorite colors to suit your personal style. The plaited cord gives a rustic, natural look.*

3 Thread this wire through the stretched coil, pulling it right up to the loop.

5 Cut a piece of black wire 1 in. (2.5 cm) longer than the butterfly. Thread on a 5 mm green wood bead and form a head pin at one end (see page 181). Push the wire through the coil, as shown.

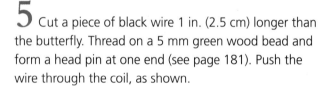

4 Thread one green seed bead onto each extended wire. Using round-nose pliers, form an open spiral at the end of each wire for the antennae. Work harden the spirals (see page 185).

6 Using your round-nose pliers, form a link at the other end of the wire (see page 180).

7 Cut a 6-in. (15-cm) length of black wire. Place the center of the wire about three-quarters of the way up the coil and wrap it around once or twice, leaving about 1½ in. (4 cm) of wire extending on either side. Thread each extending wire with about 30 black and green seed beads, leaving about ½ in. (1 cm) of wire extending on each side.

8 Using your round-nose pliers, form a small, tight spiral at each end of the protruding wires. Using your fingers, curl the beaded wires around in concentric circles to form a "wing" on each side of the central coil.

9 Decide how long you want your necklace to be and cut two pieces of cord in each color to this length. Bind all the cords together at one end with a small piece of masking tape. Secure the bound end in a vise and plait. Secure the other end with another piece of masking tape.

10 Using your round-nose pliers, make a coiled fish-hook clasp and fastener from 24-gauge (0.6 mm) black wire (see page 189). Slip the "eye" of the fastener onto one end of the cord and squeeze the last loop of the coil with your flat-nose pliers to secure. If you wish, you can add a tiny dab of Superglue onto the end of the cord for added security.

VARIATION:
Butterfly Pins

Make a jacket lapel or hat pin by threading a ready-made lapel-pin finding through the central coil. Choose color combinations to match or contrast with your outfit.

11 Slip the butterfly motif onto the cord. Slip the fish-hook clasp onto the other end of the cord and secure in the same way as the eye.

Sweetheart Necklace

Suspended from lengths of satin ribbon, this pink heart-shaped pendant is about as girly as you can get! For a more casual look, you could make the design without beads, using a thicker gauge or colored wire, and suspend it from a ready-made cord or chain. The heart motif would also look great on the front of a card or gift tag, or attached to a key ring.

YOU WILL NEED

- 20-gauge (0.8 mm) silver wire
- Approx. 60 x size 9/0 pink seed beads
- 1 x 7 mm pink bead
- 1 x 4 mm pink bead
- 2 x 16-in. (40-cm) lengths of ¼-in. (5-mm) pink ribbon
- 2 x 16-in. (40-cm) lengths of ¼-in. (5-mm) white ribbon
- Wire cutters
- Round- and flat-nose pliers
- Mandrel or cylindrical dowel approx. ½ in. (1 cm) in diameter
- Masking tape
- Superglue

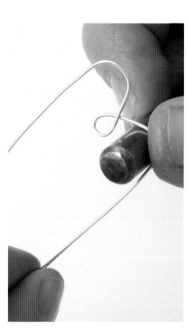

1 Cut a 6-in. (15-cm) length of 20-gauge (0.8 mm) silver wire. Holding the center with the ends of your round-nose pliers, curl the two ends of the wire around the shaft to form a loop.

2 Place a mandrel or cylindrical dowel approximately ½ in. (1 cm) in diameter just by the central loop and bring the extending wires down on each side to form a heart shape.

3 Thread each side of the heart-shaped frame with size 9/0 pink seed beads, using approximately 30 beads on each side. Using your fingers, wrap one wire two or three times around the other at the base of the heart.

OPPOSITE *Make matching earrings for a stylish jewelry set.*

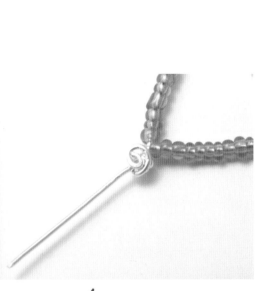

4 Snip off any excess wrapped wire and squeeze the end flat against the stem with your flat-nose pliers, leaving the other wire extending.

5 Thread a 7 mm pink bead onto the extending stem at the base of the heart-shaped frame and form a head pin (see page 181) to prevent it slipping off.

6 Cut a 6-in. (15-cm) length of 20-gauge (0.8 mm) silver wire. Place the tips of your round-nose pliers in the center and fold the wire in half.

7 Squeeze the end of the doubled wires together with your flat-nose pliers and straighten out the wires with your fingers so that they run parallel to one another.

8 Place the shaft of your round-nose pliers about ½ in. (1 cm) from the end of the doubled-over wire and bend the wire around the pliers to form a hook.

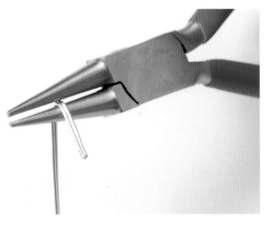

9 Thread the doubled wire hook through the center loop of the heart frame and swivel the wires around the top of the heart, curling them around your round-nose pliers so that the wires are facing down.

10 Hold the hook firmly in the jaws of your flat-nose pliers and bend it upward, until it sits against the central loop.

11 Bend the extending wires down over the heart. Holding the hook firmly in your flat-nose pliers, form a tight spiral on one extending wire (see page 182), until you have only ½ in. (1 cm) of wire remaining. Make a second spiral on the other wire, curling in the opposite direction.

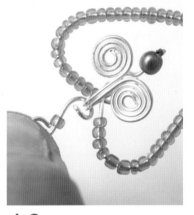

12 Thread a 4 mm pink bead onto 20-gauge (0.8 mm) silver wire, and form a head pin at one end and a link at the other (see pages 180 and 181). Connect this bead to the central loop of the heart, so that it is suspended within the frame between the spirals.

13 Using a pink seed bead, make a beaded S-link and attach it to the doubled wire loop that is at the top of the heart frame.

14 Tape the ends of the colored ribbons together and feed them through the S-link. Push the ends of the ribbons into coiled end clasps (see page 189) and secure with glue.

Bead, Wire, and Beyond

As your confidence with wire and bead has grown, you'll now want to create your own designs—perhaps taking your inspiration, as I have done in this chapter, from other cultures. Some of these projects use beads that reflect the ethnic origin of a piece or the materials that would have been available in the past, such as the bone-effect beads used in the African Dream necklace (page 168) and the Celtic Kilt Pin (page 160). Others draw on motifs or techniques that are specific to a particular culture, such as the Greek Key Bracelet (page 150), the Aztec Tree of Life Necklace (page 156), and the filigree effect of the Indian Spice Necklace (page 164). In the Nile Necklace (page 144), I've also included a method of "aging" a piece of jewelry to give it an antique feel. I hope you too will feel that, when it comes to jewelry design, the world really is your oyster!

Global Style

I've always been fascinated by jewelry from other lands, perhaps because I spent part of my childhood in Africa and was exposed to many different design influences. I'm also amazed by the way jewelry designs from the Ancient World and from civilizations that have long since disappeared can have such a contemporary feel. I hope these projects will encourage you to seek out your own sources of design inspiration.

Nile Necklace

Inspired by items found in the burial chambers of ancient Egypt, the technique used in this project is a quick yet very effective way of creating wire jewelry that has the appearance of chain mail. Experiment with different combinations of looped rows to design either rectangular or square pieces. I've "aged" the pieces by applying spray paint to create a verdigris effect like that found on old copper or bronze.

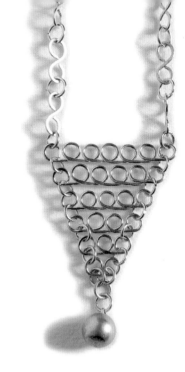

YOU WILL NEED

- 20-gauge (0.8 mm) wire
- Bead of your choice
- Round-nose pliers
- Flat-nose pliers
- Hammer and steel block
- Wire cutters

OPPOSITE
The use of the green paint on this striking necklace gives it a classic aged appearance.

1 Working from a coil of 20-gauge (0.8 mm) wire, form a small loop at one end by curling it around the tips of your round-nose pliers.

2 Reposition your pliers beside the first loop and form another loop. The top wire should twist over the lower wire in the same direction as the first loop.

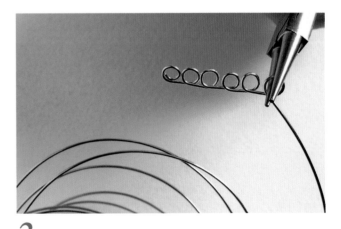

3 Continue shaping the wire into loops around the jaws of the pliers, until you have formed a row of seven complete circular loops.

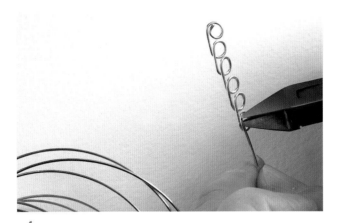

4 Using wire cutters, snip off the loops from the coil, giving you a row of loops.

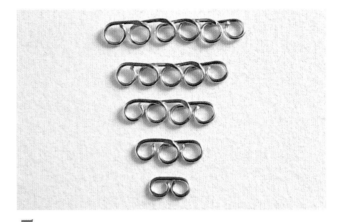

5 Repeat steps 1 to 4 to create another wire row with six circles, then make rows with five, four, three, and finally two circles.

6 Very gently flatten the pieces, by tapping them with a hammer. Be careful not to hammer where the wires cross as this will weaken the wire.

7 Make approximately 16 jump rings (see page 182). Connect all looped rows together at their ends in descending order, using 14 of the jump rings.

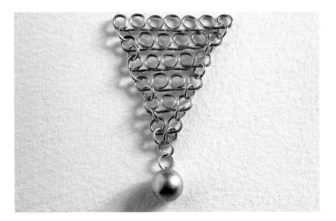

8 Join the drop bead to the base of the looped triangle, using the two remaining jump rings and the flat-nose pliers. As well as looking decorative, the weight of this bead will help the triangle to hang properly, so that the rows of jump rings will be perfectly displayed.

9 Create an S-link chain from 20-gauge (0.8 mm) wire and join it to the outer loops on the top row of the looped triangle.

10 Make an S-link fastener from matching wire (see page 186) and attach it to the end of the chain to complete the design.

VARIATION:
Nile Earrings

These matching earrings are constructed in exactly the same way as the necklace, except that they are suspended the other way around, with the apex of the triangle at the top, attached to ear wires, and embellished with drop beads hanging from the bottom row.

Egyptian "Verdigris"

Any of the projects contained in this book can look completely different by varying bead sizes, colors, and wire gauges. It is possible to purchase wires in every color of the rainbow, but alternatively, as in this Egyptian design, you can color the wire yourself. Spray paint (sold for use on cars) and enamel craft paints are available from do-it-yourself stores or hobby stores.

The verdigris Egyptian necklace design was constructed out of 20-gauge (0.8 mm) copper wire with a chain created from S-links threaded with small turquoise seedbeads. A small spiral of wire is suspended from the end of the necklace for decoration.

The earrings are also created out of 20-gauge (0.8 mm) copper wire, with decorative ends made from turquoise seed beads threaded onto spiraled wire. The tops of the earrings are created by making two closed spirals with ready-made ear-posts glued to the backs. (For nonpierced ears, clips can be substituted.)

TIP

Place the piece you wish to verdigris on an old piece of newspaper within a box. Ensure that your room is well ventilated as the spray varnish has a very pungent smell (you could do this outside in fine weather).

YOU WILL NEED

- Pale green paint
- A hard stippling brush
- Clear matte varnish spray
- Kitchen paper

1 Pour a little paint out into a container and dab the end of your paint brush in it. Stipple this paint onto your piece of jewelry, coating the entire surface.

2 Where the painted areas look too heavy, gently dab the paint off with a piece of kitchen paper. Keep adding the paint and dabbing it off until you are happy with the overall effect.

3 When the jewelry is dry and coated on both sides, finish by spraying the entire surface with a clear, matte varnish to fix the paint and prevent it from flaking off through wear and tear. Leave to dry.

Greek Key Bracelet

The Ancient Greek key design is a decorative border formed from one continuous line and symbolizes infinity and unity. Practice on a length of spare wire before using your good silver wire. It usually takes a couple of attempts to create evenly shaped geometric pieces, but once you've mastered the technique, this bracelet is an easy design to make.

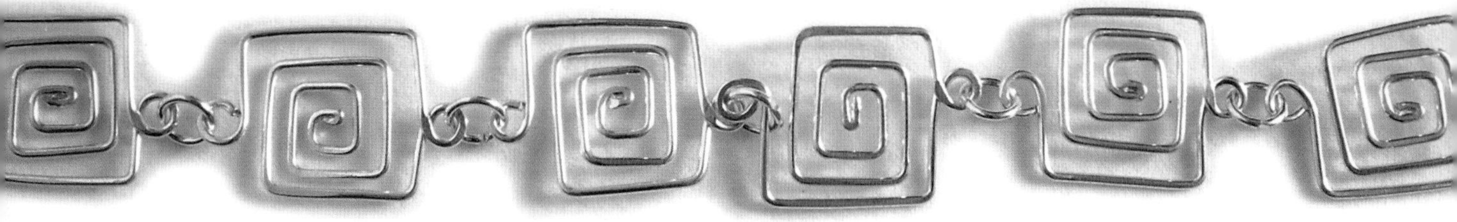

YOU WILL NEED

- 20-gauge (0.8 mm) wire
- Wire cutters
- Round-nose pliers
- Flat- or snipe-nose pliers
- Hammer and steel block

OPPOSITE *Adding a decorative bead to the chain links is a great way to customize these earrings.*

1 Depending on the size of each geometric unit, cut approximately seven 4½–5-in. (11.5–12.5-cm) lengths of 20-gauge (0.8 mm) wire.

2 With the tips of your round-nose pliers, curl the ends of these wires into tiny hooks and squeeze these flat on themselves (as you would to make a head pin, see page 181).

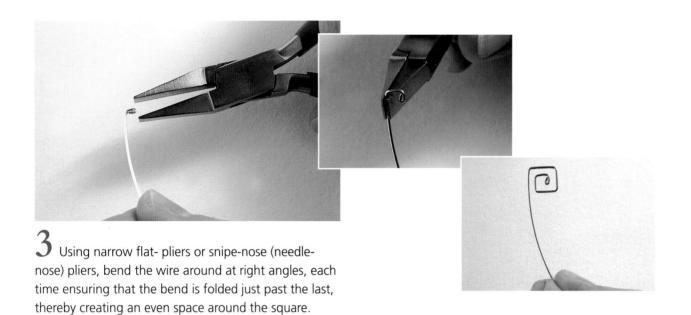

3 Using narrow flat- pliers or snipe-nose (needle-nose) pliers, bend the wire around at right angles, each time ensuring that the bend is folded just past the last, thereby creating an even space around the square.

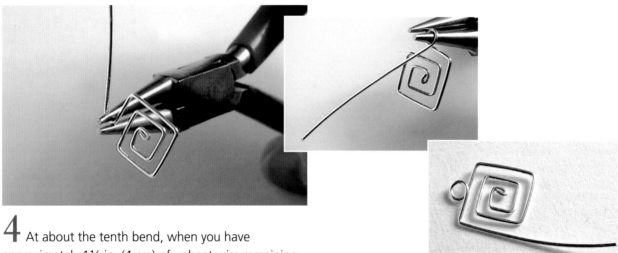

4 At about the tenth bend, when you have approximately 1½ in. (4 cm) of unbent wire remaining, form a small link by curling the wire around your round-nose pliers, crossing it over, and bringing it down to form the outer side of the square.

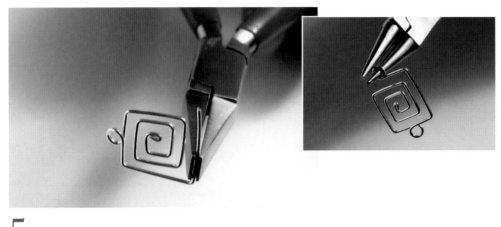

5 Create another link at the end of the wire in the same way, parallel with the cross-over link on the other side of the square.

6 Flatten and gently tap each unit with your hammer (be careful not to hammer the cross-over link or you will weaken the wire).

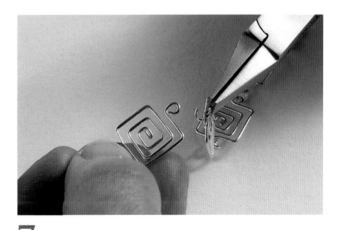

7 Attach all units together with jump rings (see page 183) and create a fastener for the bracelet in matching wire (see pages 184–189).

Greek Key Earrings

These earrings are created in the same way as the bracelet units, by following steps 1 to 6. The small suspended squares are created in a similar way, but instead of step 4 (where the wire is crossed over), just bend the wire up at a right angle, thread on a bead, and form a loop at the top to suspend the bead from your geometric unit. To complete the earrings, connect both pieces onto ear wires.

1 Follow steps 1 to 6 of the Greek Key Bracelet, creating two geometric units.

2 Fold the wire as before, using flat-nosed pliers, creating the square geometric shape.

3 Create a smaller geometric wire square following steps 1 to 4 of the bracelet, but instead of making a link, thread a bead onto the projecting wire and then secure with a link.

4 Connect this beaded unit to the geometric square and suspend from an ear wire.

VARIATION:
Talismans

The Ancient Greeks used beads painted with the symbol of an eye to ward off evil spirits and to protect themselves from harm. For an authentic touch, include "eye" beads in your jewelry.

Aztec Tree of Life Necklace

The ancient Aztec civilization inspired me to create this turquoise and gold necklace. The Aztecs were renowned for the production of vivid precious-stone mosaics, and excelled in both stone and metal work. These designs were created as tributes to the gods, with the "tree" representing the cycle of life and the use of gold symbolizing the sun. Turquoise was worn by Aztec kings and is probably one of the oldest gemstones known. It was a sacred stone to the Aztecs as it was (and is still) attributed with healing powers.

Semi-precious chip stones can be purchased from bead or jewelry suppliers in 16- or 18-in. (40- or 45-cm) lengths. You may be surprised to discover just how inexpensive they are!

OPPOSITE *The smaller turquoise beads look great fixed to the larger gold centerpiece.*

YOU WILL NEED

- 14 in. (35 cm) 20-gauge (0.8 mm) gold wire
- 12 in. (30 cm) 26-gauge (0.4 mm) gold wire
- 10–12 semi-precious turquoise drilled chip stones
- 2 x 4 mm gold beads
- Ready-made wire choker
- Round- and flat-nose pliers
- Wire cutters
- Hammer and steel block

1 Cut 14 in. (35 cm) of 20-gauge (0.8 mm) gold wire. Place your round-nose pliers in the center and bend the wire around them to form a circular shape.

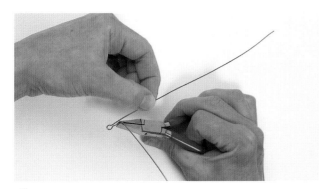

2 Straighten the extending wires so that they run parallel to each other. Hold one wire in your flat-nose pliers and bend it outward at right angles, just a little way up from the circular tip.

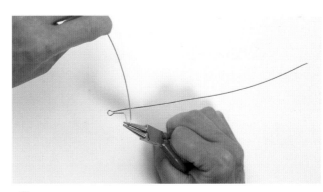

3 Between ¼ and ½ in. (0.5 and 1 cm) from the bend, fold this wire back toward the other wire, bending it around your pliers to create a curved end. This is the first "branch" of the tree. The measurements do not have to be precise: the design is asymmetrical, so just follow your instincts as the pattern evolves.

4 Straighten the wires so that they run parallel to each other again. Using your flat-nose pliers, repeat steps 2 and 3 with the other wire to form another "branch" in the same way.

5 Make three or four branches on each side, about ¼–½ in. (0.5–1 cm) long at the base, increasing to 1 in. (2.5 cm) in the center, and reducing to ¼–½ in. (0.5–1 cm) at the top. Secure the wires by wrapping one around the other two or three times.

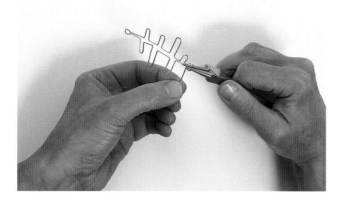

6 Form a link at the top (see page 180). Secure the extending wire by wrapping it around itself. Press firmly with your flat-nose pliers and cut off any excess.

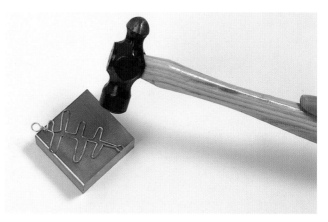

7 Hammer the tree very gently on a steel block to flatten and work harden it, making sure you do not hammer the wrapped wire end.

8 Snip off a piece of 26-gauge (0.4 mm) wire about 2 in. (5 cm) long and wrap it neatly around the top branch of the tree.

9 Thread a turquoise chip stone bead onto this wire and wrap the wire onto the wire branch below. Press with your flat-nose pliers and cut off the excess wire.

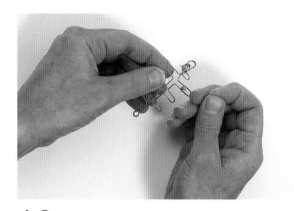

10 Continue threading stones onto the branches, wrapping the wire around as described in step 9.

11 Thread 26-gauge (0.8 mm) wire through chip stone beads; wrap one end of wire around the other to secure. Form a link. Cut off excess wire.

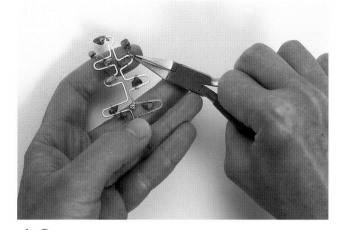

12 Make jump rings (see page 182) and attach the pendant drops to the ends of some of the branches.

13 Thread the completed tree onto a ready-made wire choker ring.

VARIATION:
Twisted Choker Ring

Make your own choker ring by twisting two or more wires together (see page 45). For a really individual gift, substitute the recipient's birthstone for the turquoise chips.

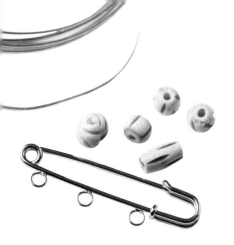

Celtic Kilt Pin

The pin was used as a dress fastening during the Iron Age and Celtic period and this modern-day pin can be used in the same way to secure a shawl, cardigan, skirt, or sarong— or simply to adorn a jacket lapel. My design features three motifs: I placed a simple and slightly elongated version of a Celtic cross in the center of the pin, with a spiral, which is one of the most characteristic and recognizable elements of Celtic style, on one side and a triangular motif that reflects the geometric designs found on wood carvings, shields, and swords on the other.

I used bone-effect beads in my design, as bone is a material that would have been readily available in Celtic times—but of course you could use any charm or colored beads of your choice.

YOU WILL NEED

- ❧ 18-gauge (1 mm) silver wire
- ❧ 3 x 8 mm round bone-effect beads
- ❧ 1 x 6 mm barrel bone-effect bead
- ❧ 1 x 12 mm cylinder bone-effect bead
- ❧ Round- and flat-nose pliers
- ❧ Wire cutters
- ❧ Hammer and flat steel stake
- ❧ Ready-made kilt-pin finding

1 First, make the triangular wire motif. Using the tips of your round-nose pliers, make a little hook at the end of a spool of 18-gauge (1 mm) silver wire. Squeeze the hook flat with your flat-nose pliers to make a head pin (see page 181).

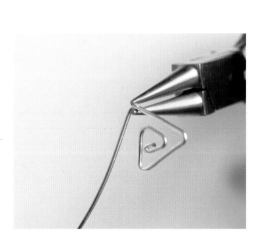

2 Place the tips of your round-nose pliers next to this head pin and bend the wire through 90°. Repeat five or six times, folding the wire just past the previous bend each time, to create a triangular shape, trying to keep the spaces between the wires even.

3 Place your flat-nose pliers in the last bend and bend the wire upward to form a stem at the top of the triangle. Cut the wire off the spool, leaving about ½ in. (1 cm), and make a suspension link at the top of the motif (see page 180).

ABOVE *The central "cross" motif gives this pin a Celtic feel, together with the triangular and circular shaped spirals on each side. If you prefer, you can balance the design by making the two spirals identical.*

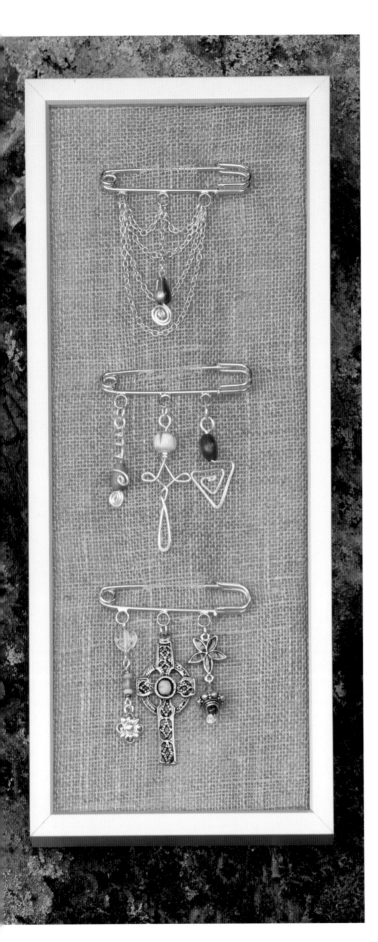

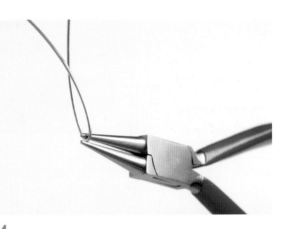

4 To make the central cross motif, cut a 6-in. (15-cm) length of 18-gauge (1 mm) silver wire. Find the center of the wire with your round-nose pliers and bring the two ends together, crossing the ends over one another about 1 in. (2.5 cm) up the wire.

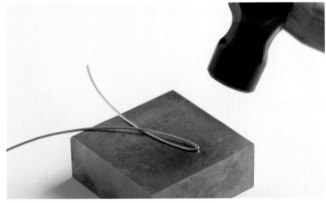

5 Hammer the base of the doubled end of the wire on a steel stake to flatten it.

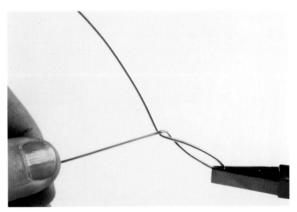

6 Twist one piece of wire around the other, just above the hammered area, to form a small loop, which will be the top of the cross motif.

OPPOSITE, FAR LEFT
Kilt pin brooches with various pendant charms— swagged chain lengths, beads, and ready-made charms. Make brooches to suit your particular style and personality.

7 Place the fattest part of your round-nose pliers on one side of the twist and form a circle, curling outward, bringing the extending wire back toward the center. Repeat on the other side to form the two "arms" of the cross. Bring the two loose ends of wire together and wrap one around the other. Cut off any excess wire and neaten the ends (see page 187).

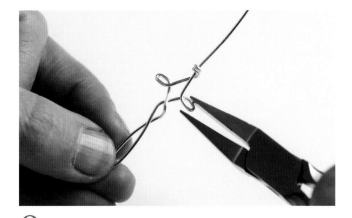

8 Squeeze the circular loops on each side of the cross with your flat-nosed pliers to elongate and flatten them.

9 Thread your chosen bead onto the top of the cross and, using your round-nose pliers, form a suspension link (see page 180) on the projecting wire. Cut off any excess and neaten the ends.

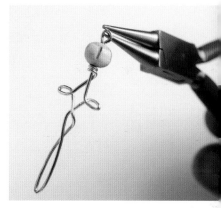

10 Working from the spool of 18-gauge (1 mm) silver wire, make an open spiral by curling the wire around itself (see page 182). Cut the wire off the spool, leaving about 1 in. (2.5 cm) extending. Thread your chosen bead onto the extending wire and, using your round-nose pliers, form a suspension link at the top (see page 180).

11 Thread your chosen beads onto the wires extending from the triangular and cross motifs and form a suspension link at each end. Make jump rings (see page 182) and attach the charms to a ready-made kilt pin.

Indian Spice Necklace

This necklace was inspired by the delicate filigree work that is characteristic of traditional Indian jewelry—in particular, the ornate forehead decorations worn by Indian brides. The colors chosen are reminiscent of the warm glow of tasty, exotic spices.

OPPOSITE *The overall effect of this necklace is very ornate and intricate—guaranteed to impress!*

YOU WILL NEED

- Approx. 60 in. (150 cm) 20-gauge (0.8 mm) gold wire
- Orange-colored and pearl 3 mm seed beads
- 15 x 4 mm pearl beads
- 18 mm pearl focal bead
- Approx. 6 in. (15 cm) ready-made trace chain
- Round- and flat-nose pliers
- Wire cutters
- Dowel about ½ in. (12 mm) in diameter

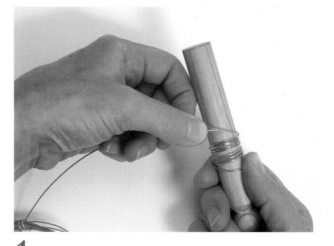

1 Working from the spool, coil the wire around the dowel 16 to 17 times.

3 Using the ends of your round-nose pliers, curl one end of five of these scallops into a link (see page 180). Thread two pearl, two orange, and two more pearl seed beads onto each curved piece and form a link at the other end of the wire.

2 Cut each circle off the coil, just as you would to make jump rings (see page 182). Using your wire cutters, snip about ½ in. (1 cm) out of one of the circles. Discard the snipped-out piece. Use the remainder as a guide to remove the same amount of wire from the rest of the full circles to make scallop shapes.

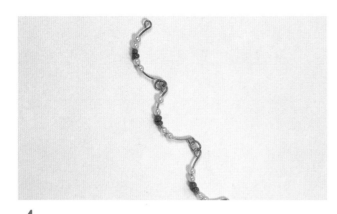

4 Make jump rings and link the five beaded scallops together to form the first row of the necklace, by connecting jump rings between the side loops.

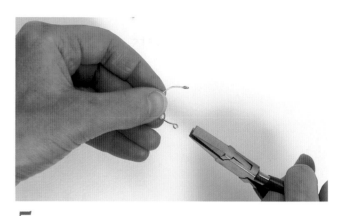

5 Thread the remaining ten scallops with seed beads. Using flat-nose pliers, twist the links at each side 90° so that they are at right angles to the row of beads.

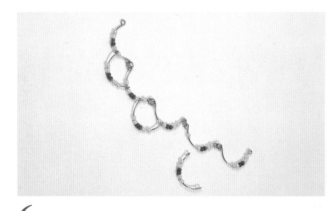

6 Link four scallops onto the first row. Place the first one between the last two pearl beads of the first scallop and the first two pearl beads of the second scallop on the top row. Continue until the row is complete.

7 Continue adding rows of beaded scallops, using one less scallop in each row so that you end up with an inverted triangle.

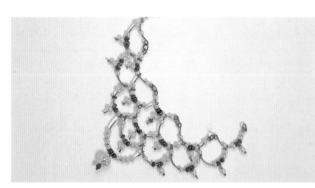

8 Suspend a threaded pearl bead from the center of each scallop. Repeat steps 2 and 3 to make a larger scalloped wire to suspend on either side of the last row, threading it with eight pearl seed beads and two orange ones, as shown, and suspend a large focal bead between the two orange seed beads.

9 Cut the ready-made chain into 1-in. (2.5-cm) sections. Thread small lengths of wire with one pearl, one orange, and one pearl seed bead. Connect the piece onto a ready-made chain interspersed with threaded beads.

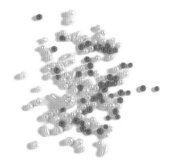

VARIATION:
Bold Color Contrasts

Strong color contrasts give the piece a very different look. Here, I substituted black and red beads for the orange and pearl seed beads and suspended a faceted black bead from the large scallop at the base. The result is much bolder in appearance and could be worn with casual clothes, whereas the "Indian" version is more formal and "dressy."

African Dream

Having spent my early childhood in Africa, I have always been inspired and influenced by African tribal art. Collared necklaces are traditionally worn to indicate status and wealth. Even though colored beads are often used, I decided to use wood and bone beads in my design as they remind me of all the wonderful traditional carvings that I have seen. The copper wire of the collar is intended to mimic the dusty red earth of the African plains.

If you have problems finding the cylindrical, carved beads, make the necklace out of suspended coils of wire (like narrow jump ring spirals) or suspend "stacks" of threaded beads from the collar.

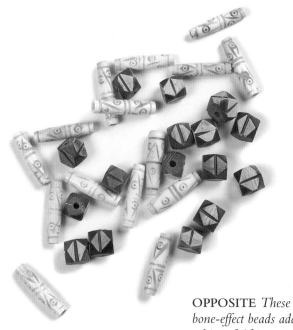

OPPOSITE *These bone-effect beads add a hint of African style to this necklace.*

YOU WILL NEED
- 17 x 20 mm cylindrical bone-effect beads
- 18 x 10 mm square wooden beads
- 36 in. (90 cm) 20-gauge (0.8 mm) copper wire
- Round- and flat-nose pliers
- Wire cutters

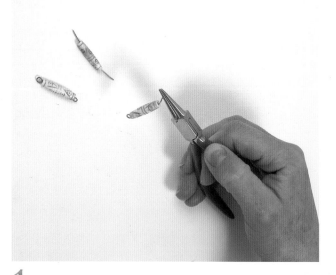

1 Thread the cylindrical beads with 20-gauge (0.8 mm) copper wire, forming a link at each end with your round-nose pliers (see page 180).

2 Do the same with the 18 wooden beads, so that each bead has a link at each end.

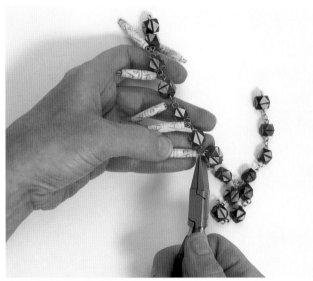

3 Connect the wooden beads with jump rings (see page 183) to form the outline of the collar necklace.

4 Undo one link on each cylindrical bead and suspend the beads from the jump rings on the collar.

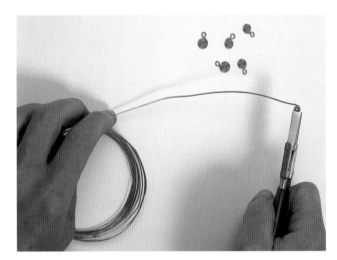

5 Working from the spool of wire, form a tiny hook with your round-nose pliers. Squash the hook with your flat-nose pliers and curl the wire around itself to form a small spiral (see page 182). Cut the wire off the spool, leaving just enough to form a small link at the end (see page 180). Make 17 spirals in this way.

VARIATION:
Earrings

To make matching earrings, link a cylindrical bead and a wooden bead together, with a copper spiral at the base of the wooden bead, and suspend from ready-made ear wires.

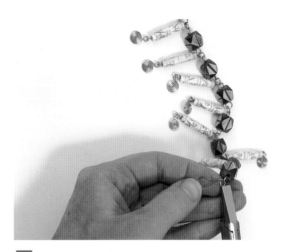

6 Connect the spirals to the links at the end of the cylindrical bone beads.

7 Make a fish-hook clasp and eye (see pages 184 and 186) and attach to the ends of the necklace.

VARIATION:
Black–Bead Necklace

This dramatic collared necklace was made from black wooden carved beads and threaded with black iron wire.

Belly Dancer's Bracelet

Dangling silver and gold coin decorations give this bracelet an exotic flavor! To make matching earrings, connect three of the looped silver units together with jump rings to form an inverted triangle, attach a pair of coin decorations to the lowest loop, and suspend the entire piece from ready-made earwires. You could also extend the bracelet into a necklace by attaching a piece of ready-made chain to each side.

OPPOSITE The contrast of the silver and gold coins gives this piece a delightfully textured look.

YOU WILL NEED

- ✃ Approx. 3 ft (1 m) 20-gauge wire (0.8 mm) silver wire
- ✃ 18 gold- and 18 silver-colored metal "coin-like" decorations about ½ in. (1.5 cm) in diameter
- ✃ Round- and flat-nose pliers
- ✃ Wire cutters
- ✃ Hammer and steel block

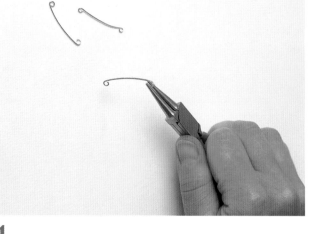

1 Cut 18 1½-in. (4-cm) lengths of 20-gauge (0.8 mm) silver wire. Curl the ends into small loops, curling them in toward each other.

2 Mold the center of the looped wire around the widest part of your round-nosed pliers, making sure that the loops curl outward. Flatten and work harden each unit by hammering it on a steel block (see page 185).

3 Make jump rings (see page 182) and connect the coins together in pairs, with one gold and one silver coin in each pair.

4 Connect the looped units into a chain, using jump rings.

5 Attach one pair of coins to each looped unit, closing the jump rings with your flat-nose pliers. Make a fish-hook clasp (see page 184) to close the bracelet.

Tools and Techniques

The next few pages provide a brief overview of the main tools and materials needed for making wire and beaded jewelry, along with the basic techniques you will need. You may well be surprised to discover just how little you require in the way of specialist skills and equipment. For most people, however, the main thrill of jewelry-making lies in selecting from the vast array of beads and wires on offer; from semi-precious stones and hand-made glass beads to mass-produced beads, there really is something to suit every occasion.

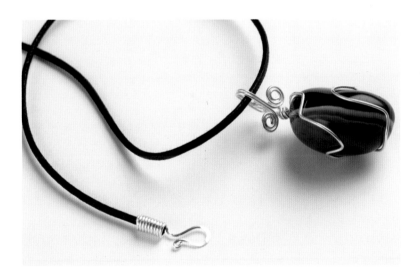

Tools

One of the joys of making wire and beaded jewelry is that you require very little in the way of tools and equipment. Although there are various specialist gadgets on the market, the items shown on these two pages are virtually all you are ever likely to need and all are readily available from craft suppliers, mail–order catalogs, and, of course, the Internet.

An added bonus is that this equipment takes up very little space and can be quickly and easily stored away in a box when it is not in use. This really is a craft that you can pursue at your kitchen table, whenever you have a few minutes to spare!

Pliers and cutters

The only really essential pieces of equipment are a good pair of wire cutters and two or three kinds of pliers with which to shape the wire. There are three types of pliers used in making wire jewelry—round-nose, flat-nose, and chain-nose. As pliers and cutters are tools that you will use all the time, it is well worth investing in good-quality products.

Round-nose pliers have round, tapered shafts, around which you bend the wire—so they are ideal for coiling and bending wire into small loops and curves, as well as for making jump rings to link units together.

Flat-nose pliers have flat, parallel jaws. They are used to grip the wire firmly as you work with it, and to bend it at right angles. They are also essential for neatening and flattening ends so that no sharp wires stick out. Unlike household electrical pliers, they are smooth-jawed, with no serrations or grips that might mark the wire. This is particularly important for enamel-coated, colored wires, because if the coating is damaged you will be able to see the copper wire core underneath, which would spoil the look of the piece.

Chain-nose pliers are similar to flat-nose pliers, but they have tapered ends. They are useful for holding very small pieces of wire and for fabricating more intricate and delicate pieces, as well as for bending angular shapes in wire.

Wire cutters are available in several forms, but I find that "side cutters" are the most useful as they have small, tapered blades that can cut into small spaces. Always hold the cutters perpendicular to the wire when cutting, to achieve a clean cut.

FROM LEFT TO RIGHT: *round-nose pliers, flat-nose pliers, chain-nose pliers, wire cutters.*

A hammer and flat steel stake used for work hardening.

Hammer and flat steel stake

These tools are used to flatten and toughen wire motifs (see page 185). You can use almost any hammer, provided it has a smooth, flat steel end, although specialist jewelry hammers are generally small and lighter than general-purpose household hammers, so you may find them easier to use.

Steel stakes can be bought from specialist jewelry stores. The surface must be polished smooth, otherwise the wire will pick up any irregularities that are present. Always keep the hammer head at right angles to the wire being hit, otherwise you will obtain a textured surface.

Mandrel

To form circular shapes such as rings and bangles, you will need a mandrel. You can buy purpose-made mandrels in varying sizes; alternatively, shape your wire around any cylindrical object of the appropriate size. Wooden dowels from your local home-improvements store are an inexpensive option. Depending on the size you need, you could also improvise by wrapping wire around a round-barreled pen, a glass jar or bottle, a rolling pin, or a curtain pole.

Materials

There is such a wonderful array of beautiful beads, colorful wires, and findings that you will be spoilt for choice! When you're making a piece of jewelry to celebrate a special occasion, however, some materials spring to mind immediately. Gold and silver wires—either plated or made entirely from the precious metal—always look luxurious, particularly for a once-in-a-lifetime occasion such as a wedding. Similarly, pearls (for weddings) and semi-precious chip stones (for birthdays or anniversaries) are obvious choices. But of course, it all depends on the occasion—and, just as importantly, on the age and personality of the person for whom you're making the piece.

Wire

Wire is available in many thicknesses, types, and colors. Colored, copper, and plated wires can be bought from most craft and hobby stores, as well as from bead suppliers. Colored wires are usually copper based with enamel coatings, which means that they must not be hammered or over-manipulated as this might cause the surface color to be removed.

With the exception of precious metal, wire is generally sold in spools of a pre-measured length.

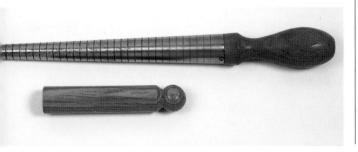

A specialist ring mandrel, marked with graduations showing standard ring sizes, and an improvised mandrel—a short length of wooden dowel.

Colored wires are available in every color of the rainbow!

Precious-metal wire is bought by length, the price being calculated by weight. Always store precious-metal wire in self-seal bags, away from oxygen, to prevent it from tarnishing. If it does look dull, rub it with a soft polishing cloth.

Instead of precious-metal wires, I almost always use gold- or silver-plated wires, which are far less expensive and, in the case of silver-plated, will not tarnish so quickly. The only exception to this is if

you need to file the wire, as filing will expose the copper core underneath the coating.

All these kinds of wire come in different thicknesses. Depending on where you buy your wire, different measurements are used to denote the thickness of the wire. The chart below will enable you to convert quickly from one system to another. The most commonly used general-purpose wire is 20-gauge (0.8 mm).

26-gauge	0.4 mm	Binding, knitting, and weaving
24-gauge	0.6 mm	Threading small delicate beads; binding and twisting
20-gauge	0.8 mm	General-purpose jewelry work
18-gauge	1.0 mm	Chunkier pieces and ring shanks
16-gauge	1.2 mm	Bolder, chunkier jewelry
14-gauge	1.5 mm	Very chunky, metallic wire jewelry

Copper-, gold-, and silver-plated wires are less expensive than the precious-metal versions but look just as convincing.

Glass beads range from completely transparent to almost opaque. They can be expensive, particularly if they are made from hand-blown glass, so it is perhaps best to use them as "focal" beads for maximum impact.

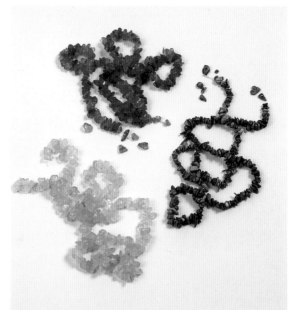

Seed beads are usually sold in small tubes. They are useful as "stopper" beads but, because they are so tiny, if you want them to have any impact in a design you generally need to string several together. The size of a seed bead refers to the number that will fit into 1 in. (2.5 cm) when laid end to end—so the higher the number, the smaller the bead.

Semi-precious chip stones are sold in 16- or 18-in. (40- or 45-cm) lengths. When you are ready to use them, snip the thread that holds them together and store the beads in small containers. Again, these are lovely beads to use for jewelry for special occasions such as birthdays and anniversaries, as you can match the bead to the recipient's birthstone and create a piece that is not only aesthetic, but also symbolic.

Beads

Beads are made from all kinds of materials including glass, porcelain, plastic, metal, wood, and bone. Specialist bead stores contain literally thousands of different sizes and types, arranged by both color and size, and I defy anyone to visit such a store without buying a selection!

Always check that the wire you are using fits through the bead hole, as there is no correlation between the size of a bead and the diameter of its hole.

If you can't find beads that match those used in the projects in this book, buy something of a similar size. You will also find that many bead suppliers sell mixed colored bead bags at wholesale prices. These are often great value!

Findings

Findings is the jewelry term used to describe ready-made components such as chains, ear wires, fasteners, and so on. They can be bought from craft and hobby stores. If you are using a ready-made chain in a design, make sure you check that the links are large enough to take

whatever thickness of wire you use to thread or suspend the embellishments. It is possible to buy ready-made jump rings, fasteners, and head pins, but you can create your own by following the instructions in the basic techniques section, using wire that matches the rest of your project. This is also a less expensive option!

Ready-made findings come in a wide variety of colors and finishes.

Basic Techniques

If this is your first attempt at wire jewelry, practice all the basic techniques to become familiar with the fundamentals of wire working and get a "feel" for your main ingredient—wire. You may find it all a bit fiddly to begin with, but you'll soon get the hang of it. Start with 20-gauge (0.8 mm) wire, as it is a good general-purpose wire that you will probably use a great deal.

Threading beads with wire and forming links

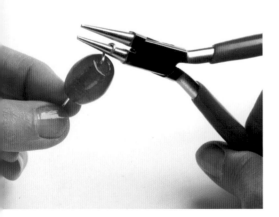

1 Working from the spool, thread your chosen bead onto the wire, leaving about ½ in. (1 cm) of wire extending on each side of the bead with which to form the link.

2 Remove the bead and cut the wire with your wire cutters.

4 Hold and squeeze the very end of the bent wire tightly with your round-nose pliers and curl it toward you into a circle. It is better to do this in several short movements than to attempt to make one continuous circle. Repeat steps 2–4 to form another link at the other end of the bead.

3 Thread the bead back onto the cut wire. Holding the wire vertically, with the bead in the center, use the tips of your round-nose pliers to bend the wire at a right angle, at the point where it touches the bead.

At the end, hold each link firmly in the jaws of your pliers and twist until both links face the same way.

180

Making a head pin

If you want to suspend a bead from a chain, you only need a suspension link at one end of the bead. At the other end, you need to make what is known as a "head pin," which is virtually invisible but prevents the bead from slipping off the wire.

The head pin is unobtrusive but prevents the bead from slipping off the wire.

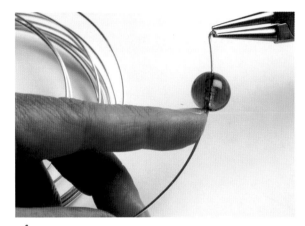

1 Working from the spool, thread your chosen bead onto the wire and let it slip down, leaving the end exposed.

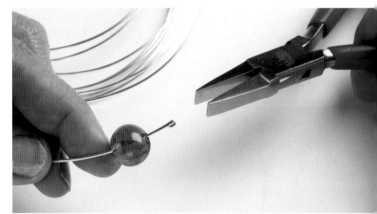

2 Using the tips of your round-nose pliers, make a tiny curl at one end of the wire. Squeeze this curl flat with your flat-nose pliers to create a knob of wire.

3 Push your bead right up to the "head pin" and snip the wire leaving a stem of about ½ in. (1 cm) and form a link at the other end using your round-nose pliers. If the hole in the bead is large and it slips over the head pin, bend the head pin at a right angle, so that the bead sits on top of it like a tiny shelf. (Alternatively, slide on a small seed bead to act as a stopper.)

You can also make a decorative feature of the head pin. To do this, you need to leave a longer length of wire below the bead. From left to right: wire curled into a closed spiral; wire hammered into a "feather" shape; seed bead threaded onto the wire above the head pin.

In an open spiral, evenly spaced gaps are left between the coils.

Making spirals

There are two kinds of spiral—open and closed. Each is formed in the same way, the only difference being whether or not any space is left between the coils. Both types of spiral begin by curling a circle at the end of the wire.

A closed spiral is made in the same way, but has no gaps between the coils.

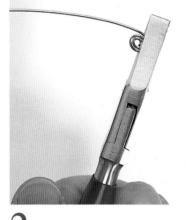

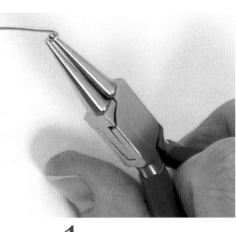

1 Begin by curling a small circle at the end of the wire, using the tips of your round-nose pliers. Try to make this circle as round as possible, as the rest of the spiral will be shaped around it.

2 Grip the circle tightly in the jaws of your flat-nose pliers and begin curling the wire around it. For a closed spiral, shown here, butt each coil up tightly against the previous one. For an open spiral, leave space between one coil and the next, making sure that the spaces are even.

3 When the spiral is the size you want, leave about ½ in. (1 cm) of wire to form a suspension link, curling the projecting end of wire into a small loop in the opposite direction to the spiral.

Making jump rings

Jump rings are used to connect units together. You can buy them ready made, but it is well worth learning how to make them yourself as you can then match the jump ring to the color and size of wire that you are using. It is also much less expensive to make them yourself!

Jump rings are made by forming a wire coil around the shaft of your round-nose pliers, out of which you snip individual rings as required. When you bring the wire around the pliers to begin

forming the second ring of the coil, it needs to go below the first coil, nearer your hand. This keeps the wire on the same part of the pliers every time. If you bring the wire round above the first ring of the coil, the jump rings will taper, following the shape of the pliers' shaft.

You can also make jump rings by wrapping wire around a cylindrical object such as a knitting needle, a large nail or the barrel of a pen, depending on the diameter that you require.

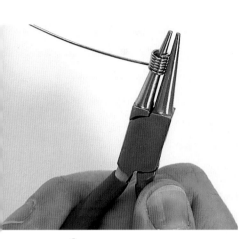

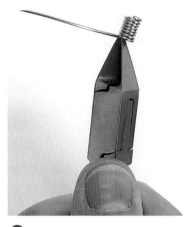

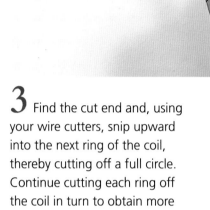

1 Working from the spool, wrap wire five or six times around one shaft of your round-nose pliers, curling it around the same part of the pliers every time to create an even coil.

2 Remove the coil from the pliers and cut it off the spool of wire using your wire cutters.

3 Find the cut end and, using your wire cutters, snip upward into the next ring of the coil, thereby cutting off a full circle. Continue cutting each ring off the coil in turn to obtain more jump rings.

Using jump rings to connect units

Using your flat-nose pliers, open one of the jump rings sidewise (like a door), so that you do not distort the shape. Loop the open jump ring through the links of the beads and close it with flat-nose pliers. To toughen (or work harden) the jump rings, carefully move the two ends of the ring just past one another (holding one side with your flat-nose and the other side with your chain-nose pliers); this will provide tension, enabling the cut ends to sit more securely together. Spend a little extra time checking that there are no gaps between your links, so that when you come to wear the piece you can be sure that it won't all fall apart as the beads work themselves loose. (I speak from bitter experience!)

Jump rings can also be linked together to create a chain. From top to bottom: silver jump rings linked together; copper jump rings interspersed with pairs of smaller silver jump rings; copper jump rings.

Fish-hook clasp

The most commonly used clasp is the fish-hook, which is also one of the simplest to create.

This hook-shaped clasp is both decorative and functional.

1 Working from the spool, curl the end of the wire into a loop using your round-nose pliers. Reposition your pliers on the other side of the wire and curl the wire in the opposite direction to form the fish-hook clasp. Cut the wire off the spool, leaving about ½ in. (1 cm) extending, and form a link (see page 180).

2 If you wish, you can gently hammer the hook on a steel stake to work harden (see right) and flatten it slightly, thereby making it stronger and more durable.

Doubled fish-hook clasp

As a double thickness of wire is used, this fastener is much sturdier than a basic fish-hook clasp. You will need to cut at least 3 in. (7.5 cm) of wire.

2 Using your round-nose pliers, squeeze the folded end of the wires together and straighten them out with your fingers, so that they run parallel to one another.

1 Find the center of the wire and bend the wire around the tips of your round-nose pliers.

184

3 Leaving about 1 in. (2.5 cm) of doubled wire, wrap one wire two or three times around the other. Snip off any excess wrapped wire, leaving the other stem extending.

4 Curl the doubled wire around the shaft of your round-nose pliers into a hook shape. Again using your round-nose pliers, curl the tip of the hook up into a small "lip."

5 Complete the clasp by forming a link at the end of the single protruding wire. (For extra color and decoration, you can add a bead before forming your link.)

6 The double thickness of wire makes this a much sturdier clasp for necklaces and bracelets—particularly if they contain relatively heavy beads that might put a strain on an ordinary clasp.

Work hardening

To create wire jewelry without the aid of solder, you must know how to work harden, or toughen, your material so that it can take the strain of being worn without distorting or falling apart. One method is to hammer the piece on a steel stake. The stake must be clean, smooth, and dent-free, or the wire will pick up irregularities.

Place your piece on the stake and "stroke" hammer it, ensuring that the flat part of the hammer comes down at 90° to the piece. It is easiest to hammer your piece standing up, as this ensures that the hammer head hits the wire squarely, rather than at an angle, which could creating texturing and "dimples" in the metal. After hammering the piece several times, you should notice the wire flattening and spreading.

Be careful when work hardening colored wire as the colored coating can rub off, exposing the copper core. Use a nylon hammer or place a cloth over the piece before hammering.

This technique is not suitable for small jump rings and links, as it will distort their shape. To strengthen jump rings, take one end in one pair of pliers and one end in another and gently push them just past the point at which they should join. Do this two or three times; the piece will be work hardened just enough to hold the join without the aid of solder.

S-shaped clasp

If you'd like a clasp to look rather more decorative, an S-shaped clasp is a good option.

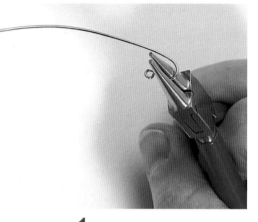

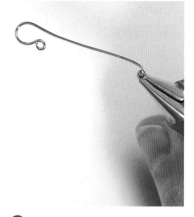

3 Place the widest part of your pliers just under the loop and mold the wire around the shaft in the opposite direction, to create a mirror image to the first curve and complete the S-shape.

1 Working from the spool, curl a tiny loop at the end of the wire, using the tips of your round-nose pliers. Place the widest part of your pliers just under the loop and curve the wire in the opposite direction.

2 Cut the wire off the spool leaving a 1-in. (2.5-cm) stem. Make a small loop at the other end of the wire, curling toward the "hook" that you have just created at the other end.

Adding a bead before you form the second curve of the S-shape makes an attractive variation. Wire it on each side with 28-gauge (0.4 mm) wire to prevent it from slipping.

The "eye" of the fastener

This "eye" can be used to complete all the clasps shown above.

1 Working from the spool, curl a piece of wire around the widest part of your round-nose pliers about 1 in. (2.5 cm) from the end of the wire to form a loop, crossing the end of the wire over itself.

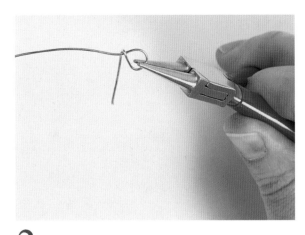

2 Wrap the extending wire around the stem, just under the loop, to secure. Squeeze the cut end flat against the stem with the tips of your chain-nose pliers, to ensure there are no spiky, protruding ends.

3 Cut the wire off the spool, leaving about ½ in. (1 cm) extending. Using the tips of your round-nose pliers, form the extending wire into a link (see page 180).

4 Gently hammer the rounded end of the "eye" on a steel stake to flatten and toughen it. Do not hammer the wires that have been wrapped over the stem or you will weaken them.

The completed "eye" of the fastener can be linked to the ends of a necklace or bracelet, either directly or via jump rings.

Neatening ends

When you've wrapped one piece of wire around another—as when making a clasp, for example—it's important to neaten the ends to prevent any sharp pieces from sticking out and snagging on clothing or scratching the wearer.

Simply snip the wire as close as possible to the stem, and then press it firmly with your flat- or chain-nose pliers to flatten it against the piece of jewelry.

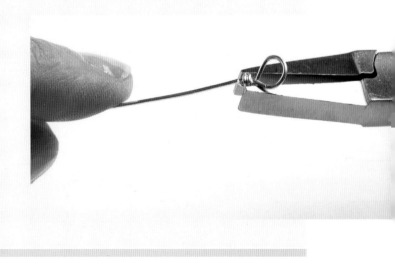

Beaded eye clasp

For a more decorative fastener, incorporate a bead in the "eye." You can use the same technique of wrapped loops when threading large beads to make the links more secure.

1 Working from the spool, thread your chosen bead onto the wire. About 1 in. (2.5 cm) from the end of the wire, bend the wire at right angles around the shaft of your round-nose pliers, so that it crosses over and forms a little loop.

2 Wrap the short end of the wire two or three times around the stem. Neaten the ends (see page 187).

3 Bend the wire at the other end of the bead at right angles, as in step 1.

4 Wrap the wire around the shaft of the pliers to form another loop.

5 Holding the loop firmly in your flat-nose pliers, wrap the wire two or three times around the stem. Cut the wire off the spool and neaten the ends.

As a finishing touch, work harden the links (see page 185), taking great care not to hammer the bead.

Coiled fish-hook clasp and fastener

This is a variation on the basic fish-hook clasp. It is used on cord, rope, or ribbon—in fact, on anything to which a jump ring or hook cannot be attached.

1 Working from the spool, make two coils of wire about ¼ in. (5 mm) long, in the same way as when making jump rings (see page 182). Remember to check that the cord or rope you are using can fit snugly into the center of the coil.

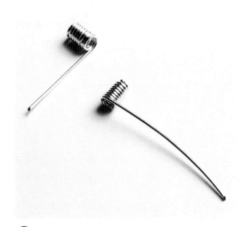

2 Cut the wire off the spool, leaving a 1-in. (2.5-cm) tail of wire on one coil and a 1½-in. (4-cm) tail on the other.

3 At the end of the longer wire, form a fish-hook clasp (see page 184) without a suspension link. Using your flat-nose pliers, turn the hook at 90° to the coil.

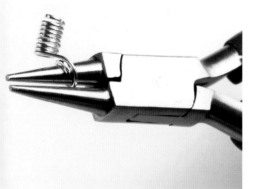

4 At the end of the shorter wire, curl your wire around the widest part of your round-nose pliers so that it sits perpendicular to the coil, thus forming the eye of the fastener.

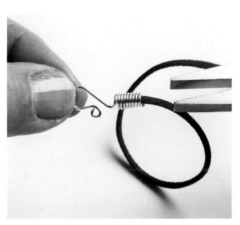

5 Insert the cord or ribbon into the coil. Press the last ring of the coil tightly against the cord with the tips of your flat-nose pliers, so that the fastener is held securely in place.

The completed coiled fish-hook clasp and fastener. For added security, I recommend dabbing some Superglue just inside the end of the wire coil.

Celtic Cross jig pattern
(page 22)

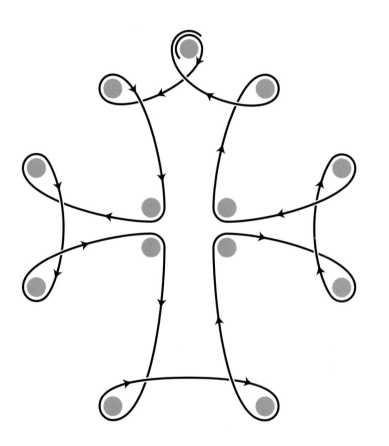

Suppliers

UNITED STATES

CGM Inc.
19611 Ventura Boulevard
Suite 211
Tarzana, CA 91356
Tel: (800) 426 5246
www.cgmfindings.com

Fire Mountain Gems
1 Fire Mountain Way
Grants Pass, OR 97526-2373
Tel: (800) 355 2137
www.firemountaingems.com

Jewelry Supply
Roseville
CA 95678
Tel: (916) 780 9610
www.jewelrysupply.com

Land of Odds
718 Thompson Lane
Ste 123, Nashville, TN 37204
Tel: (615) 292 0610
www.landofodds.com

Mode International Inc.
5111-4th Avenue
Brooklyn, NY 11220
Tel: (718) 765 0124
www.modebeads.com

Rings & Things
P.O. Box 450
Spokane, WA 99210-0450
Tel: (800) 366 2156
www.rings-things.com

Rio Grande
7500 Bluewater Road. NW
Albuquerque, NM 87121
Tel: (800) 545 6566
www.riogrande.com

Shipwreck Beads
8560 Commerce Place Dr. NE
Lacey, WA 98516
Tel: (800) 950 4232
www.shipwreckbeads.com

Stormcloud Trading Co.
725 Snelling Ave. N
St. Paul, MN 55104
Tel: (651) 645 0343
www.beadstorm.com

Studio Galli Productions
P.O. Box 14257
San Francisco, CA 94114
Tel: (408) 828 8350
www.gallifilms.com
(DVDs only)

Thunderbird Supply Company
1907 W. Historic Rte. 66
Gallup, NM 87301
Tel: (800) 545 7968
www.thunderbirdsupply.com
(Online sales only)

Unicorne Beads
404 Evelyn Place, Suite D
Placentia, California 92870
Tel: (800) 833 2095
www.unicornebeads.com

Wig Jig
24165 IH-10 West,
Suite 217-725
San Antonio, TX 78257-1159
Tel: (800) 579 9473
www.wigjig.com

CANADA

ABG Jewelry & Accessories
20 Steelcase Road, W. Unit 1A
Markham, ON L3R 1B2
Tel: (416) 226 5762
www.abeautifulgift.ca

Bead & Craft
Tel: (888) 855 2323
www.beadandcraft.com
(Online sales only)

Bead Box Inc.
17-B Cartier
Pointe-Claire, QC H9S 4R5
Tel: (514) 697 4224
www.beadbox.ca

The Beadery
446 Queen Street West
Toronto, ON M5V 2A8
Tel: (416) 703 4668
www.thebeadery.ca

beadFX Inc.
Unit 2, 19 Waterman Ave
Toronto, ON M4B 1Y2
Tel: (877) 473 2323
or (416) 701 1373
www.beadfx.com

Bedrock Supply
9435-63 Avenue
Edmonton, AB T6E 0G2
Tel: (780) 434 2040
www.bedrocksupply.ca

Canada Beading Supply
12B-210 Colonnade Road South
Ottawa, ON K2E 7L5
Tel: (613) 727 3886
www.canbead.com

UNITED KINGDOM

Burhouse Beads
Quarmby Mills, Tanyard Road,
Oakes, Huddersfield
West Yorkshire HD3 4YP
Tel: 01484 485100
www.burhousebeads.com

Cookson Gold
49 Hatton Garden
London EC1N 8YS
Tel: 020 7400 6508
www.cooksongold.com

Creative Beadcraft
Unit 2, Asheridge Business Centre
Asheridge Road
Chesham
Buckinghamshire HP5 2PT
Tel: 01494 778818
www.creativebeadcraft.co.uk

Jilly Beads Ltd
1 Anstable Road
Morecambe
Lancashire LA4 6TG
Tel: LA4 6TG
www.jillybeads.com

The Scientific Wire Co.
Unit 3 Zone A
Chelmsford Road Industrial Estate
Great Dunmow
Essex CM6 1HD
Tel: 01371 238013
www.wires.co.uk

Wirejewellery.co.uk
Tel: 01732 850727
www.wirejewellery.co.uk
(Author's website)

Index